Help Your Savings: Money Management for the Unemployed

Michael R. Grenier

MRG Web Creations

DISCLAIMERS

1. Information from websites was used in this book. Although the author attempted to use legitimate and reliable websites, he does not accept any responsibility for the accuracy of the data. He merely reported it.

2. Additionally, actual websites are specifically mentioned in the text of this book. The author has no affiliations or interests in connection with in any of these websites other than his own (www.helpyoursavings.com). The author does not recommend any websites over any other, whether mentioned or not, and all comments about any website are based solely on his experiences as typical user.

3. This book presents information to help reduce expenses based on the author's own experiences and information reported from other sources. The author makes no claims as to any specific savings, or whether his suggestions will result in any savings. It is up to the readers to determine, using common sense, whether to employ any or all of these suggestions based on their own situations. The author assumes no responsibility for the actions of the readers in regards to this book.

4. In matters regarding health, health care, and prescription medications, the author is not a doctor and makes no assumptions about any reader's health. Readers are advised to speak with their doctors before changing any prescription or non-prescription medications, including but not limited to amounts, dosage, or brands. Readers retain responsibility for their own health related decisions.

CONTENTS

AUTHOR'S NOTE

The idea for this book occurred to me in the middle of one of my many sleepless nights while I was unemployed. As I lay there in bed staring at the time projected on the ceiling from the alarm clock, it occurred to me that it's possible to save money by making minimal efforts, and that much more money could be saved with greater effort. It was the formation of what I call "The Tiers." I got all worked up over it. Unfortunately my enthusiasm died by morning and it was replaced with fatigue from lack of sleep. When I thought of it later during the next day, it seemed to be a dumb idea.

A funny thing happened though. The idea kept coming back to me. Maybe not nightly but often enough that I remembered what I had already thought, and I added more ideas to the mental stew. But during the day, when dealing with my job search and other life events, thoughts of the book diminished. Again my idea didn't seem so wonderful.

Eventually the idea crept into my mind during the day. That's when I decided to take the first step: I created the rough outline for the book. The next step was a biggie: I decided to tell someone about it. Naturally I chose my partner. I still was afraid he'd politely say it's a good idea, but I should focus on other things – like getting a job. After much hesitation, I discussed the concept of this book with him. I was surprised when he proclaimed it great idea that I should pursue.

Once I started work on the book, I mentioned it to other friends. I was certain some would tell me it was a good idea no matter what they thought, and others would be brutally honest and tell me it was a stupid idea. None told me that writing this book would be folly, and their enthusiasm was high, so I pressed onward and completed it.

Therefore I wish to thank my dear partner, Michael M, for his guidance, assistance, enthusiasm, discipline when I didn't feel like writing, and his love and compassion. A huge thanks to Jenifer O. for her edits, suggestions, and support. I also thank Janet M. for her insight and suggestions, Alene S. for her taking the time to thoroughly think about the project before finding it a worthy effort. The list continues with Bob P., Runar P., and Marsha B., and Glenn S. for their honest questions and encouragement. I also thank Gretchen M. for her unending support, and another dear friend, Lou D., for his financial expertise and unending friendship.

I have true wealth with such people in my life; thank you so much.

INTRODUCTION

Thanks for buying this book. I'm glad you did. Not because of the sale I just made, although I won't refuse it, but because I'm delighted to know that you are making a step to help yourself through a difficult period – your unemployment. The point of this book is to help you manage your money while you're out of work; in other words, to make it last and to avoid falling into debt until you get your next job.

I would recommend that you get other books or access other resources to help you get that next job. There are tons of books out there to help you with your resume, how to knock them dead at your interviews, and how to find that perfect job. This book won't help you with those things, but it will help you manage your money plus give you a few things to think about.

The Initial Slap

You may or may not have seen it coming. You get yourself to work one morning and you go through your normal routine. At some point you are called into your manager's office or the human resources department and you're told that your services are no longer required. Thanks but no thanks. Adios. Au revior. Goodbye. There's no negotiation. There's no goodbye lunch or party. You might even be escorted out the door, stripped of your security badge, your keys, and your dignity.

You may have felt you were slapped in the face and then thrown into the wild alone. All I can say is that you're justified if you feel, hurt, angry, and scared. Even if you hated the job, you still maybe would have liked it to end on your terms, not theirs.

I've been there, and more than once. Funny how it doesn't get easier each time. Who likes to be told that you're no longer needed? Nobody. But here you are without a job. And if you think you're going to get sympathy from me, you're absolutely right! Like I said, it's happened to me, so I know all the feelings all too well. Go ahead: punch those pillows, have that cry, spend a day or two watching reruns of Gilligan's Island, whatever you need to do to cope and get those feelings past you.

But once you get over that initial sting and mix of feelings, the next thing to do is to start a course of action. Even if you've been unemployed for a while, it's still not too late to make some plans.

The Initial Steps

The first thing you might want to do is to develop a plan for finding that next job. Your unemployment office might help you with that, as might any number of books on the topic. Get encouragement from friends and family, and take all necessary steps to help you become employed again.

At the same time, you also need to take that other initial step: Look at your financial condition. For some this may not be a big deal, and for others, you might be as fearful as opening the closet door when you know there is a fire-breathing monster waiting to come out and eat you.

Here is where the sympathy stops. You've got to get a handle on your finances. The reason is very simple: You and maybe your family need to live, eat, and be sheltered during your period of unemployment, and those things all require money. Although the sympathy stops, my desire to help you continues. And you have my assistance to financially guide you through this transitional time.

So after you've cried in your beer or coffee, take out those bank statements and checkbooks because it's time to take charge of your money. I can hear some of you saying, "Ha! My savings consists of $10. This is hopeless…" Whether you have $10, $100, $1,000, or $10,000 in the bank, you can benefit from this book because it's about stretching each dollar to the maximum. It's also about how to avoid debt as much as possible. So if you only have $10 in the bank, okay, that's a challenge. But keeping your expenses lower creates less debt. Remember, the smaller the debt, the quicker you can pay it off once you're back in the workforce.

And for those of you who have $10,000 or more in the bank, think about how long it took you to save that amount compared to how long it will take you to spend it. If you want to make that $10,000 last for your whole unemployment period and hopefully have some left over after you get hired, then you'll need to manage it.

In either case, $10 or $10,000 in the bank, I can help you. Granted, it may not always be easy, but you can do it. I know you can.

The Four Parts

This book is broken down into four parts. Part I is no more important than what's in Part IV; I just broke it down into sections for convenience. I won't be offended if you start with any part because all of the contained information is to help you.

Part I is the main reason for this book. In it I discuss all major expenses we normally have to pay. For each expense, I give you three levels, or tiers, by which you can save. The first tier is the easiest to implement, but will save you the least amount of money. To enjoy the increased savings of the second tier, more effort is required. The highest tier is for those who want or need to really cut expenses to the maximum. I leave it up to you to decide which tier you want to use, but regardless which you use, you will save money. And the more money you save, the longer your nest egg will last, or the less debt you'll incur.

Part II offers a valuable tool to implement sound money management. It's called a budget. You don't need to be Albert Einstein or have a degree in finance to create and use a budget, but you'll be much financially smarter with it in place.

Part III discusses other ways to save money, avoid money pitfalls, and offer alternative ways to get what you need. These cost saving strategies didn't lend themselves to the "tiers" so they got their own section in the book.

Part IV gives you more things to consider while you're unemployed, and pointers to help you continue manage your money once you get back to work.

Self-Proclaimed Expert

I can hear some of you asking, "Who is this self-proclaimed expert?" Self-proclaimed? I'm not sure. Expert? Yes. Although my degree is in computer systems management, I have a minor in accounting and economics. Most of my computer experience was supporting financial applications, and my second career as a commercial real estate appraiser was to analyze budgets, expenses, and income on proposed and existing income-producing properties. As you can see, I never ventured very far from basic accounting processes.

In reality, I knew how to manage money even before I went to college. It was a way of life for me. My parents were each the youngest of seven, and they were both born in the late 1920s of immigrant parents. Both grew up during the Great Depression of the 1930s. Both sets of grandparents had similar menial textile mill jobs and were in the same economic class: dirt poor. Their similarities ended there. My mother's parents understood the concept of money management even though they hardly had a spare penny. My father's parents didn't. Mom never went without shoes, heat, clothes, or proper food. By his own admission, Dad often went to bed hungry.

It stands to reason that Mom was the one who managed the money in our family. She had excellent teachers – her parents. She also imparted this wisdom to me, for which I will be eternally grateful, for it was one of her best gifts.

Through most of my growing years, money was very tight. Dad made a very modest salary and Mom stayed at home to raise my sister and me. By experience and by necessity, she was able to make every dollar stretch to a $1.10 or more. Bills were paid on time, we never went without any necessity, and other than an occasional car loan and a small mortgage, they were completely debt-free. Mom had an excellent way of budgeting (see more about this in Part II), and she was very disciplined. She taught me early on the importance of having savings and the value of a dollar.

Later on in life, I didn't always practice the fine art of budgeting every penny in my life. I was making a decent salary and always participated in 401K plans and various other savings plans. I also joined the ranks of the millions who made mistakes with credit cards and learned firsthand how difficult it is to pay them off. Fortunately, my mistakes were minor compared to many. After finally paying those off, I vowed never to let that happen again, and fortunately I've held true to the promise.

The biggest advantage I had was living well below my means. It always made me very nervous to spend a lot of money for anything, so I rarely did it. That's not to say that we didn't go on vacations or enjoy life, but I was always careful about it and didn't over-indulge. When I got laid off, it wasn't a big deal to move back to my savings mode. As a matter of fact, it was very easy for me; it was second nature.

This second nature is what I'd like to impart with you. It doesn't mean the end of the world; it just means a different approach to money and to your spending habits. Remember, it's temporary, but if you're savvy, you'll keep these good habits after you get that next job.

Take the Plunge

It would be nice to have a crystal ball that would tell us how long we'll be unemployed. Making decisions about money would be much easier. Unfortunately, there is no such crystal ball, but you might have some sense. Your job function, skills and the demand for them, and other factors, such as willingness to relocate, should give you an indication of whether this will be a short or long term period of unemployment. But even that's not a sure thing.

So please look through this book to find out how you can make your finances work for you during your unemployment. You've already purchased this book, so you might as well get your money's worth from it. Start reading and start saving!

PART I – SAVING ON THE TIERS

"Saving money" has two meanings: 1) To actually put money in the bank, and 2) to reduce expenses. The first builds your capital, and the second preserves it. Both require effort because let's face it, it's much easier to spend than to save. In an ideal world, as when you're employed, you can do both. You can take a percentage of your salary and put it into some sort of savings account before you start paying any bills or expenses. This is called paying yourself. Then by watching your expenditures, you are saving money by paying less for products and services. Really smart people know how much less they pay, and put that "savings" into the bank. For example, if the register tape at the supermarket says "Your total savings today is $12.56," they will deposit that amount into their savings account. Those of us who can practice both meanings of "saving money" will certainly come out ahead.

But you are unemployed and putting money into the bank is probably no more of a reality than flying to the moon for a weekend. If you are unemployed and are actually able to cover your expenses and put money into your savings account, then you don't need this book, – I applaud you! But the rest of us need to focus on the second definition of "saving money," which is to reduce expenses. Paying less for things means your money will last longer, or it means you avoid will falling deeper into debt.

Just as it takes effort to put money into the bank, it takes effort to reduce expenses. We live in a world centered on convenience, but convenience comes at a high price. While working, we may not have had the time or energy to seek the best deals, so we would opt for convenience. Now that we are unemployed, we need to cut expenses. We have the time to do so.

Like everything else, the harder you work at cutting expenses, the more you will save. In this part, I discuss typical expenses and give you ways to cut the amount you pay for them. Some require little effort while others may force you to do more work. At the end of each expense I summarize these cost-saving measures by grouping them into three levels which I call Tiers: Moderate, Motivated, and Extreme.

Moderate: If you want to save some money, but are not willing to drastically change your ways, then the Moderate Tier will work best for you. You'll save money, guaranteed. But this tier saves you the least amount of money because it requires the least amount of effort and sacrifice. This tier offers a great starting point to help you preserve your capital.

Motivated: This tier tightens the belt a few more notches. You'll realize more savings than the Moderate Tier by putting in more effort. The effort doesn't necessarily mean hard labor, but rather research from either the internet or phone calls. It also requires planning and being conscious of every dollar you spend. This tier does not mean a radical change in your lifestyle even though it forces you into new habits regarding money management.

Extreme: As the name implies, this tier does mean change and sacrifice. It will also give you the most savings. You should consider The Extreme Tier if you have little savings left or have to use credit cards to pay bills.

Which tier you use is entirely up to you and your comfort level. By the way, there is nothing that says you can't mix and match the tiers. There is also nothing to stop you from using two or even all three tiers, although sometimes tiers will be mutually exclusive, meaning that it's not possible to combine them. Whatever method you use is entirely up to you. After all, you know your own situation better than anybody else.

I invite you to read the whole book, but if you're like me, you might only want to read the sections that pertain to you. So for your convenience, I've labeled all the sections in this part to make it easier for you. For example, if you rent your home, you can easily skip the section on mortgages and go directly to the section for renters. Maybe sometime down the road the material in the mortgage section will help you, if you buy a place of your own.

So take a few minutes and look through the topics, find the ones that pertain to you, and start your plan of action.

FOOD

Everybody needs to eat every day and that includes those of us who are unemployed. When you're out of work, you've got to sustain your body and your mind, because let's face it, looking for a job is hard work. But there is room for savings. Because you invested in this book, you've at least considered changing your spending habits. Let's start with grocery shopping.

Sometimes we get set in our ways. When we were working, our minds were preoccupied with the job, which took up at least 8 hours of each day. Then we would think about things such as picking up children from soccer practice, walking the dog, preparing dinner, and on and on. So we would shop where we had been shopping for the last hundred years. We would sometimes use coupons, provided we didn't leave them on the countertop at home. And we would have certain foods that we would automatically buy each week. In other words, everything about food shopping was habitual because we didn't have the time or energy to rethink the process. Frankly, it was low on the priority list, and justifiably so. A layoff has changed things, and it's a good opportunity to now rethink grocery shopping. This chapter helps you, borrowing a term from the corporate world, "re-engineer" your food shopping process. First we'll discuss where to shop, then we'll consider using coupons. Finally we'll end the chapter by examining what we buy. The point is to change your habits to achieve the greatest savings. Incidentally, bulk or club stores are discussed in Part III – More Savings and Pitfalls.

Supermarkets are dangerous places for the weak-willed and hungry. Everything about them is designed to make you spend your money. The produce is enticingly laid out under spotlights and glistening with fresh water droplets from the misting system. The aisle ends have appealing imported products such as Italian pasta, French cheeses, and other gourmet items. Clerks pull stock to the front of the shelves so you won't miss your favorite box of cereal. The deli and bakery sections offer enticing aromas to lure you to buy their rotisserie chickens and fresh baked breads. And to make you spend even more money, many supermarkets stage demonstrations on how to prepare certain meals and offer free samples. Is it any wonder that many of us carry a few extra pounds more than we should?

Most of the items are low-priced (as compared to a furniture or electronics store), so the impulse is to buy more than you intended. You may think, "Heck, this looks really good and it's only $2.99; big deal," and into the cart it goes. Well here's some food for thought: If you make 10 such decisions in one trip to the market, you've spent $29.99 plus any applicable taxes on top of your already high bill. What percentage of your unemployment benefit does that $30 represent? If yours is similar to mine, that comes to about 11%. Putting it into perspective, you've just pulled another $30 from your hard-earned savings because let's face it, it's almost impossible to live solely on unemployment compensation. So, take a breath and let your rational side guide you to resist spending more than you need. The battle is on: You vs. the mighty supermarket chains. But here's some good news – you can win!

Where to Shop

We are a society of labels. You are what you wear. You are where you socialize. And you are where you shop. That was fine when you were working and had the income to support that. Now is the time to change that mentality, and especially where you shop for food.

Boutique markets: Without naming any of these chains, these are the stores that offer a wide variety of produce, conventional and organic; fresh fish, chicken and meat cut and sized to order; huge selections of fine cheeses, wines, and other luxury items. These stores are extremely popular because you'll find all kinds of wonderful foods you wouldn't find at your regular supermarket chain. Typically when I venture into these stores, I end up with two brown bags, made of recycled paper complete with handles, and I'm out at least $100. Even when I was working and making a good salary, my thrifty instincts screamed at me to stay out of these stores.

Now that your income has been temporarily reduced, it may be time to consider shopping elsewhere, at least until you're back at work. There is no doubt that such markets are highly appealing, but they are also very expensive in comparison to traditional supermarkets. A savvy shopper would only use boutique markets to buy items unavailable any place else, and only if needed and justified. The bottom line is that an apple is an apple; realistically speaking, it won't taste any different from the one you buy at your local Safeway, and your wallet will thank you.

Chain or traditional supermarkets: These are everywhere: Safeway, Krogers, Winn-Dixie, Publix, Hannafords, to name a few. Most tend to be regional, so the selection of stores depends on your area. For example, where we live, I get to choose between Publix, Winn-Dixie, or Albertson's.

Nonetheless, there are usually two or three chains in most areas, so that works to your benefit because they are all competing for your dollars.

Supermarkets have large floor spaces to carry huge inventories of food, pharmaceuticals, wine and liquor, health and beauty aids, household cleaners, and seasonal items. And in some you'll even find sections dedicated to organic items. They have very efficient distribution systems, use proven food storage methods, and have direct access to food processors. The result of this huge investment and high real estate is lower prices with a good selection.

Most of these chains produce weekly circulars that are delivered to you either by mail or in the newspaper as inserts, with more modern delivery methods via websites. Many of us put these flyers directly into the recycle bin or trash without a second look as we sorted the mail between the important and the junk. It's time to reclassify some of the junk into important – those circulars.

Circulars show what's on sale for the week. And that means savings for you, so take a look at them; it's worth it. It's not a huge time consumer, because most of the circular are pictures. Look for items you use. Look for buy-one-get-one-free promotions. In my case, I look at the circular online the morning of the sale. I look for things I normally buy or close substitutes. I look what's on sale for meats and base my menus on that. And sometimes where I shop makes it even easier by providing menus complete with recipes. Best of all, usually tucked in a corner of the last page, you may find a coupon for a significant amount of money off your total bill provided you spend more than a certain amount. I frequently see a coupon for $5 off the total if it's more than $50. It's not hard to spend that much, and $5 in my pocket is better than theirs.

Big-box stores: These are supercenters that combine supermarkets with department stores. My experience with these, particularly Wal-Mart, can save you money, but they don't have the same wide selection as regular supermarkets. They also tend to let their shelves run out or low before restocking, which could lead you to buy more expensive items as a substitute. Despite that, if you can stomach the crowds, these stores can help you save on your grocery bill provided you stick to your list. And if you're there to buy food, stay out of the rest of the store because the temptation to pick up something else will completely offset your savings, or worse, make you spend more.

Shopping on the Tiers:

Moderate
Stay out of the boutique markets and shop at the traditional supermarkets.

Motivated
Watch the circulars for all markets in your areas. If the competing markets are reasonably close, buy sale items at one, and finish your shopping at the one you prefer.

Extreme
Shop at the supercenters. Find low-cost substitutes for the brands or items that are not stocked in these stores.

Using Coupons

Coupons are a great way to save money. Many smart shoppers use them all the time, not just when there is a squeeze on the pocketbook. You can think of it this way: It's free money. All you have to do is snip a few rectangles of paper and remember to take them with you when you go shopping!

Most stores will accept manufacturers' coupons as well as their own. Manufacturers' coupons are the ones you find in the Sunday paper; the manufacturer will reimburse the owners of the market for the value of the coupon when your buy that particular product. Supermarkets don't get reimbursed for their own coupons.

A few months ago I saw a sign at the checkout where I usually shop. It said, "We accept coupons from these competing stores" and it listed most of the supermarkets in the area. Check your favorite market's website, or better yet, ask the cashier if your market has a similar policy. They may not advertise it, but they'll tell you if you ask. If yes, this is a bonanza for you, so check all of the circulars, not just where you normally shop. If not, then check competing markets if they have such a policy because this may be a reason to switch. And especially keep an eye out for those coupons that offer dollars off your total order. That's even more free money with hardly an effort. I look for those $5 off the total order coupons from competing markets and use them where I normally shop. They are accepted without a hassle.

Although the practice seems to be waning, some chains will still double your coupons, usually under a dollar. It's worth checking if markets in your area still offer that feature. But check the overall pricing structure of the market because some offset the "savings" with higher pricing for all other items.

In some parts of the country, all you have to do is mention that a competing store has a better price, and they will match it. No need to clip coupons, or even show the competitor's circular. All you have to do is open your mouth. I can't guarantee that will work everywhere, but it's certainly worth asking.

There are some cautionary words about coupons though. First, make sure the product listed on the coupon is something you will use and not something you *think* you'll use. There is a difference: The "thinking" part indicates a chance that whatever you bought will end up getting pushed to the back of your pantry where it'll be forgotten and eventually tossed because it expired, or you finally decided against using it. There is no saving here; you just wasted your precious money.

Second, be careful of the terms of the coupons. Some require you to buy two or three packages to get your savings. That's fine if you know you'll be using all of them in the near future. You don't want to be buying things for the distant future when you'll be working again because by then, buying groceries won't be as difficult.

Also, don't get fooled by the savings. For example, a 50 cents off coupon for Brand A's jar of mustard sounds good, but when you get to the market and you see Brand A sells for $2.99 and Brand B, a close substitute, sells for $1.99, what's the better deal? In this case you're better off leaving the coupon on the shelf for someone else and buying Brand B.

Keep your eyes open for coupons. Sometimes they are right on the product you're buying, neatly folded and taped to the lid or side of the box. Many supermarkets have automated coupon dispensers in the aisles, and some stores even print them on the back of your receipt, or as a separate handout. Some come in with your mail; don't be hasty to classify those heavy envelopes as junk mail any more. Open them and take a look in case there is even a single coupon you can use. Then, there is Sunday paper, so loaded with coupon inserts that they fall out all over the place. This is not my first choice for coupons because 99% of them are for products we don't use. My shopping tends to be heavy on the basics because I do my own cooking. I found that it wasn't worth dishing out $2 for the paper when I was only getting a 20-cent coupon. As for the paper itself, I didn't read it.

Another place to look for coupons is from websites. Many stores make their circulars available online. They also have a neat feature which allows you to make your grocery list by clicking on the items, and then you can print the coupons on your own printer. Be careful though because some sites print one coupon per page. Think about what paper costs, and more importantly, toner cartridges or inkjet refills. Be smart; look at the circular online, make your list on a scrap of paper, and when you get to the market, take a circular from the kiosk and clip your coupons there. Why should you pay printing costs on coupons?

For those of us who are firmly entrenched in the internet age, there are sites which do nothing but offer coupons. Coupons.com, SmartSource.com and Savings.com are just a few. Some offer coupons aimed mostly for food and household products where some offer savings for department stores, services, and even luxury items.

I experimented with three websites which centered more on food and household products. All three worked in the same way: Click on a category, select the coupons to print by "clipping" them, and then click on the print icon. All three sites require software to be downloaded and installed which allow the coupons to be printed, and they all give you the option to register with the promise of additional savings. Of the sites I experimented with, Coupons.com seems to be the best. The site has been around since 1998 and appears to be the most straightforward. I did run into a snag: The coupons weren't printing and I had a vague message telling me I had to uncheck this "Keep printed documents" option. This is a printer setting which allows you to quickly reprint documents directly from the printer; it doesn't destroy the source document from your computer. I had to research that option and how to change it, and once I did, I was able to print the coupons. It was only after I started closing windows that I found instructions from Coupons.com on how to change that printer setting; the instruction box was a "pop-under," meaning it didn't show up on the top window. At this point I had already solved my printing issue, and it's just as well because the instructions were for Windows XP only, there were none for Vista or Windows 7. If you're not computer savvy, I would recommend that you have a friend help you out with that issue.

SmartSource.com is another site I examined. This one works very much like Coupons.com, but has fewer coupons. The printing software installed itself on my computer's desktop; not the ideal place. And when I clicked on a coupon and then the print button, I got a full-page ad with an offer to visit the manufacturer's website. It was only afterwards that I realized I didn't actually click on a coupon; it just looked like one. Caution is the keyword for this site; make sure you know what you're clicking on. Unwanted recipes also printed with my coupons; a waste of both paper and toner.

The last site I tested was Savings.com. This one is geared to all kinds of savings, not just groceries. I was unable to install its "print activator," the software to print their coupons.

A word of warning is warranted for some, or many, of these sites. Be very cautious. There are many coupon sites that may not be legitimate. First, before you register, read the terms and agreement. Also look at the privacy policy. I was appalled on one popular site by the amount of data they collect: credit card information, transaction history, demographics, etc. I decided my personal information is worth more than the few coupons, so I refused to register. And on unknown websites, you could put yourself at serious risk when you install their software. You could be installing more than just the ability to print coupons. Bundled in that "printing" software might be spyware, which are programs that snoop and collect information about you, your credit card data, and potentially passwords. Be wary and be smart: Research those coupon sites before you register and/or download any software.

Finally, there are dozens of books out there on the fine art of coupons. These may be a way to get additional money-saving coupons, so by all means check these out. Just don't let "couponing" become too much of an addiction because, after all, you should be spending most of your time seeking employment or a way to bring in some income.

Coupons on the Tiers:

Moderate

Clip coupons from the circulars at your favorite supermarket. Plan your meals and your shopping based on the specials and coupons they offer for the week. Don't forget to look for the valuable coupon offering money off from your total bill.

Motivated

Clip coupons for most or all markets in your area if they are reasonably close. If your market accepts competitors' coupons, you've got it made. Otherwise split your shopping between two stores, but don't waste gasoline and your time just to save 35 cents at the second store. Clip coupons from the Sunday paper, and always keep an eye out for more.

Extreme

Get into the habit of gathering manufacturers' coupons. Scan all circulars for more coupons, and, if needed, split your shopping between three or more markets keeping in mind your time and gasoline costs. Join websites dedicated to coupons and purchase books on the subject.

The Foods We Buy

We've considered where to shop and using coupons, now let's examine the food going into the cart. This is a difficult subject because it's subjective. What is good food to me might be considered deplorable by someone else. You may find the quantity I consume as being too much or too little. I am not a doctor, nor is this book about nutrition; it's about saving money. Unfortunately, I can only offer broad guidelines on this topic because I can't account for everybody's eating habits, health concerns about food, or tastes. But a degree of common sense is applicable, and that's what I'll focus upon in this section. If you find that your diet is not something you care to adjust for whatever reason, please skip this section. I won't be offended.

'Tis the Season: Did you ever look for blueberries in February? If you found some, would you have called the price a bargain? Probably not, because they weren't in season. If you looked for them in August, when they are in season, you could have gotten four times the amount for maybe less than February's tiny package.

Buying fruit and vegetables when they are in season is a huge savings. Stores offer lower prices because growers and distributors are overflowing with produce. You pocket the huge savings. And not only are these items cheaper, they are also fresher and healthier.

My Plate Runneth Over: The easiest way to save on your food bill is to simply reduce the quantity. Ask yourself if you frequently end up tossing food into the trash or disposer. If so, then there was too much food on the plate. Reducing is easy because you're not changing what you normally eat, the way you cook, or even the frequency. It just means looking for that smaller package when things are sold by weight.

For example, boneless chicken breasts typically sell for $4.99 per pound in my area, and there are usually three to the package. Look for the package of smaller breasts and this will save you up to $2.00. Or go for the largest ones and cut them in half, and get two meals out of the one package; that's an even bigger savings. In either case, if you get complaints about people still being hungry, increase the quantity of the cheaper side dish, like rice or vegetables.

The Runner Up: Anyone who does the household food shopping and/or cooking has their favorite brands, either because they taste better, work better in recipes, or has become an automatic response. Well, now may be the time to rethink those more expensive brands, at least while you're not working. Begin with the more painless items, like sugar. Is it going to matter if you use the store brand verses the national brand? Seriously, will anyone notice?

Granted there are products where I would be the first to admit that store brands are inferior to the leading seller. But by what degree? We are fortunate that we live in a society where there are plenty of laws regulating the quality and labeling of food, so even though a particular brand may be inferior, it's probably not going to be awful. Remember, it's about making the money you have last, and that does require sacrifice. I'm not going to advocate buying the cheaper brand on everything, but I am advising you to consider the alternative for each item you normally buy. Depending on the product, the difference could be as little as 20 cents to as high as a couple of dollars, and it all adds up when you've got a cartload of groceries.

Substitution is not just restricted to cheaper brands. When buying poultry, consider the price difference between light and dark meat. Less expensive cuts of beef or pork do not necessarily mean there is a sacrifice in taste, but rather a difference in how they're prepared.

If you frequently serve "meat and potatoes" as meals, there is a huge potential for savings here. Cuts of chicken and meats are among the least cost effective meals to prepare. How about substituting some of those meat-based meals with casseroles or stews? They still contain meat, but less of it, and you can get away with cheaper cuts to boot.

Speaking of poultry, did you ever consider buying a whole chicken? A whole chicken sells for much less per pound because it's less work for the processor. You can cut a chicken into drumsticks, thighs, wings, and breasts. Use what you need for a meal and freeze the rest. Don't throw away the bones and unwanted parts because those make a delicious home-made stock.

My personal preference is to cook our meals rather than buying prepared foods. In doing so, I control the levels of salt, fat, and chemicals such as preservatives, artificial ingredients and colorings. When everyone in your household was working, preparing meals from scratch may have not been possible because there just wasn't enough time. Now lack of time is no longer an obstacle to preparing at least some meals. Why not try saving some money and substituting some home-cooked food instead of chemical-laden prepared foods that are high in fat and sodium?

Another form of substitution is to go with meatless meals one or two days of the week. Let's face it, the meat section is the most expensive part of the grocery store. We all need protein, but it's also available in other foods, such as legumes. Beans are an excellent source of protein, not to mention fiber and other key nutrients. And a pound bag of beans costs less than $2! So maybe a bean dish is not what you would serve company, but think of all the things you can make with beans: Soups, chilies, casseroles, or baked beans.

Depending on your palate and your tolerances, you can bump the substitution principle up another notch. Going with generics and store brands exclusively can save you quite a bit. How much you can tolerate is entirely up to you. If you and your family have the determination, then by all means go for it. Not everyone can. For the most part, I would recommend making the value-based decision on a product-by-product basis. If you think you'll be able to eat it, try it. If you know you'll hate it and probably throw it away, then don't. There's no point in spending $2.00 for something you'll end up throwing away just to save 49 cents.

Further substitutions could include using ground beef, cold cuts and hot dogs, pasta, cheese-based dishes, and other such prepared foods. These are relatively inexpensive albeit not the most nutritious or healthy. With good judgment, however, it's possible to make some hearty meals, particularly with ground beef and/or pasta.

The amount you and your family are willing to substitute depends upon your financial situation, how long you think you'll be without an income, your tastes and tolerances, and your values. Radical changes in diet can cause problems with some people with health issues. We all know the risks involved with eating foods high in fat and sodium. It is up to you how you much you want to alter your eating habits, but keep in mind that while you are unemployed it's important that you retain your good health.

The cutback: This principle involves more motivation because it means doing away with some foods; in other words, going without. An easy target is junk food. When I shop, I'm always amazed at how many aisles have nothing but junk food, albeit named snacks or sweets. I've never bought much of this; I wasn't raised that way. When I was a kid, if anyone was hungry in the middle of the afternoon, we ate an apple. But not everyone has my approach to junk food, and to be honest, I do indulge on a limited basis.

As good as it tastes, that bag of chips, that box of cupcakes, and the bottles of soda all add up, and quite quickly. When you're watching your pennies, would you buy a boat when you don't live anywhere near water, truck tires when you don't own a truck, or a power tool when you have no desire to build anything? No, of course not, because you don't need those things. In terms of junk food, the bottom line is this: You don't need it either. Try giving it up, or at least sharply cutting back. You'll reduce your grocery bill, and maybe even reduce your waistline in the process. What an added bonus!

The "A" list: Be smart and make a list of what you **need** before going to the supermarket. And be even smarter by sticking to it. Granted, you'll probably miss something you need, and you'll see it in the aisles. That's okay; go ahead and buy it. But if you're looking at something that's not on the list, and you know you don't need it, then leave it on the shelf. Stick to that list!

You might be tempted to buy something that's on sale. "Wow, that's a really good price!" you might say to yourself. "I could use that." The key word "could" in all likelihood will translate to "probably won't." Even on sale, it's still a waste of money if you're just going to put it in the pantry and never use it. Buy it if the key words are "need" or "will use," then that's a different story.

Foods We Buy on the Tiers:

Moderate

The easiest and least painful way to save on the grocery bill is to simply cut back on the quantity. With meats and poultry, look for smaller packages, or buy the larger package and cut the portions in half. Avoid buying items when they're not in season.

Motivated

Substitute meats and poultry with cheaper cuts. Make casseroles or stews which use either less meat or cheaper cuts. Use beans to prepare meatless meals a few times per week. With planning and care, there is no need to sacrifice tasty dishes.

Extreme

Aggressive measures include forgoing products like junk food or anything other than the basics. Buy generics and store brands as much as possible. Make a shopping list and stick with it.

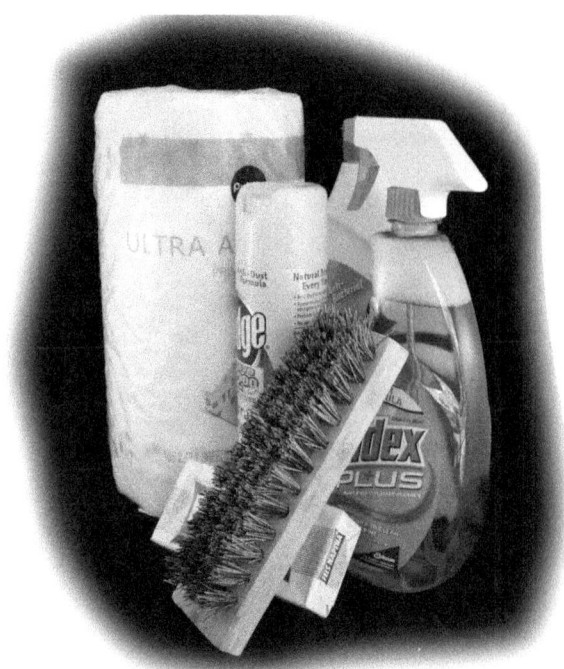

Household supplies and cleaners

Supermarkets have several aisles of cleaning and household products for our convenience and for their sales figures. That's fine. We're probably all accustomed to buying many of these products while we're food shopping. It stands to reason – we were busy and didn't have time to make a separate trip just for cleaners. There's no reason to stop buying household products at the supermarket, but maybe it's now time to look at additional flyers from the discount department stores. Stores like K-Mart, Target, and even Wal-Mart compete against supermarkets when it comes to household supplies and cleaning products. Look at their sale circulars because it may be worth the trip – provided you don't buy anything else while you're in there.

Dollar stores also sell cleaning products. Sometime they stock familiar brands as well as obscure or unknown brands. Although dollar stores typically sell food and cosmetics, many people do not feel comfortable buying these products there. However most would agree that if we don't eat it or wear it on our skin, then we're more apt to buy products from dollar stores. Certainly this applies to cleaners and other household supplies. It may be worth checking out a couple of these stores.

If we heeded all the ads for cleaners, we'd have a stockroom full of products. Laundry detergents, dish detergents, floor cleaners, tub and tile scourers, toilet bowl germicides, glass cleaners, etc. If we look under the kitchen sink, there's probably a small fortune in these products. But how many of these are necessary?

Cleaning your home is important for health and safety reasons, not to mention making you feel good about being in it. But cleaning products are expensive, so what's the compromise? Really, no compromise is needed. It's possible to get by with a fraction of those cleaners. For household cleaning, a bottle of a pine cleaner, a can of scouring powder, a bottle of bleach, and a spray bottle of glass cleaner are all you usually need. The pine cleaner is great on floors and walls, and can even be used to remove stains on carpets. Scouring powder works great on sinks and toilets; and for heavy stains, use bleach. Glass cleaners containing ammonia are actually multi-surface cleaners and can be used on faucets, counter and stove tops, and even tile floors. Read the labels of your cleaning products. In addition to instructions, you may find additional uses thereby eliminating the need for other specialized and expensive products.

As for laundry, you'll still need detergent, but that bottle of pine cleaner works great to remove oil and grease stains from clothing; just pour it directly on the spot and throw it in the washer. When that bottle of laundry pre-cleaner is empty, don't replace it, use the pine cleaner instead. Also ¼ cup of regular vinegar in the rinse cycle may eliminate the need for fabric fresheners or softeners.

For those looking to save even more money, there are dozens of websites with instructions and recipes to make your own cleaners and detergents. Most of these recipes call for ingredients like ammonia, borax, and basic soaps which can usually be found on the bottom shelf in your market's cleaning aisle. These homemade cleaners usually cost a fraction of their commercial equivalents, plus they tend to be easier on the environment. If you're interested, do some research on websites such as eHow.com, housecleaningcentral.com, or eartheasy.com.

Household supplies and cleaners on the Tiers:

Moderate

Check the ads for discount department stores for cleaners and household products. Don't exclude dollar stores for these types of things.

Motivated

As they are emptied, replace cleaners with multi-purpose or multi-surface cleaners. Why pay to have three or four products when one will do all jobs?

Extreme

Make your own cleaners. For products you can't make, buy closeouts or off-brands.

PERSONAL CARE

Health and Beauty Aids

As a society, the U.S. spends billions each year on cosmetics, grooming, and health products. Just open your medicine cabinet or your vanity and take a look; we all have dozens of bottles, bars, and boxes of "stuff" to make us look and feel better. If we think about it, that inventory probably represents several hundred dollars' worth of purchases. Granted they were probably not done at the same time, but still, you can't deny the investment. But now that we've got a temporary issue with limited income, there's probably ample room to save a bundle as we replace what's been used up. This is not to say that I'm encouraging women to walk out the door without make-up or men to go without shaving or deodorants. We must continue looking our best because we'll be going on interviews and we never know when we might be speaking with a future boss.

Beauty Aids: This category includes hygienic products like soaps and deodorants, shaving supplies, nail and skin care, hair shampoos and conditioners, cosmetics, etc. These products aren't cheap: The manufacturers and retailers know that these products are important to us and that we'll keep shelling out the money for them. Keeping in mind our financial condition, however, let's discuss some ways to save money and still keep ourselves looking good.

Whatever you do, avoid paying full price for any of these products. As with groceries, an easy way to save money on grooming products is to use coupons. Please refer to the Using Coupons section under the FOOD chapter for a detailed discussion on where to get money saving coupons. Also watch for sale circulars from department stores and pharmacies such as CVS and Walgreens.

Another simple cost saving measure can save you up to 50% on each product: Use half of what you normally use. We all tend to squeeze a full palm of shampoo or cover the whole length of the brush with toothpaste, but that's overkill, and the excess in both cases goes right down the drain. Ads for these products show beautiful people pouring rich shampoo into their hands. We see pictures of striped and gleaming toothpaste piled high on the bristles. Instead of getting our cues for how much to use from ads, we should read the small print on the package. In most cases, we end up using way too much. It's not necessary to measure or weigh the amount we use; but making a conscious effort to use only half of what we normally do will mean the product will last twice as long. This may not work with everything, but it will for most products.

If you really want to save, there are always the store brands. We all know that store brands are not always 100% as good, but if you're looking to save money, using store brands will save you some. After all, this is a time of sacrifice. And you always have the option of using dollar stores to buy some of your cosmetics.

As you use up a particular product, ask yourself some easy questions: Can one product replace two or three others? Is there a cheaper alternative? Do you need to replace this particular product?

Health Aids: This section discusses non-prescription products that you can buy in any pharmacy, whereas prescription drugs are covered in the Prescriptions section in the HEALTH chapter. These types of products range from antacids to zinc oxide, including dietary supplements. They are intended to alleviate common symptoms; in other words, they help you feel better without a trip to the doctor's office.

First, let me clearly state that I am not a doctor, and I do not have any medical or pharmaceutical training. I am not making any assumptions about your health because you are the one who knows your body and your health issues better than anybody else. You are also the one who knows your family members' health. So, if you are currently using over the counter medications either based on your doctor's advice or because from past experiences you found they worked, then please continue to do so. This section is aimed at people who are experiencing occasional minor ailments or common symptoms and are otherwise healthy. Healthy or not, however, if you think you have a serious condition, then by all means consult your doctor.

That being said, if you have a minor ailment, such as poison ivy, a bee sting, occasional heartburn, or a sunburn, then there are over the counter remedies that may help you. If I notice or feel something not quite right with my body and I can identify the problem and/or source, I will first look through my medicine chest, and if I don't already have a product for it, then I'll go to buy something. Although my doctor would not mind my visiting him, my wallet would. Why would I pay $35 for my co-pay when I know that I can get a $5 product to solve the problem? If the condition or the symptoms don't go away, then I'll make that appointment. However, if you are uncertain whether your ailment is minor, I would say to err on the side of caution and seek professional help.

When you're at the pharmacy or grocery store to buy healthcare products for a particular condition, look for the smallest package. Yes, it's a better value if you buy the larger bottle or tube, but not if you end up throwing away the unused portion five years down the road. Some products even come in "trial" or "travel" sizes. If you think that will be enough, then buy it. Now is not the time to buy larger sizes just because you think you'll need them in the future. Exceptions would be for products you use on a regular basis and you know you'll use up in the very near future.

If we take a look in our medicine chests or cabinets, I'm sure we'll all find partially used bottles and tubes of products that have long expired. These are the result of past ailments where the products either didn't work and we tried something else, or the product actually worked and now we have the leftovers. As far as the expiration dates are concerned, there are two schools of thought on this. The first is that the product, under normal storage and usage conditions, is guaranteed to work as it should until the printed or stamped date. Over time, the chemical composition may break down and the product may not work as well, or it may not work at all. Some people view the expiration date as a safety measure. The other school thinks that the expiration date is nothing but a ploy by the manufacturers to make you buy more of the product. Personally, I think the truth probably lies somewhere in between. I have no problems using health products, particularly if they are topical, well beyond the expiration date. I have used a corn remover that was ten years beyond the expiration date and it worked as it should. Conversely, I've also tried other products that simply didn't alleviate the symptom, and it wasn't much beyond the expiration date. Again, it's your health and your ailment – you decide whether you try the expired product to save the cost of the replacement, or whether you think your health is more important than the savings.

For products you use on a regular basis, keep your eyes open for sales and coupons. If you need to use it, then why not look to save yourself some money. As with beauty products, many times there are store brands as an alternative. These are packaged to look similar to the brand name and are frequently placed directly next to it. I would suggest at least comparing the labels and checking the active ingredients. If the brand has a patent, then the store brand will have similar ingredients and/or amounts, but it won't be exactly the same. Again, it's up to you. Personally, I make a product by product judgment as to whether I'll pay for the brand or save with the generic. I will, however, look for coupons and know where to buy the brand name for the least amount of money.

Health and Beauty Aids on the Tiers:

Moderate

Look for sales and coupons for the products you normally use. If you think you have a minor health issue, you may try an over the counter remedy before going to see your doctor. Buy only what you need and look for the smallest package available.

Motivated

Use generics and store brands for health and beauty aids. If you feel comfortable doing so, try using the expired product before running out to replace it. For grooming and beauty products, try using half the amount you normally do.

Extreme

Find substitute products that can replace two or three others, such as one bottle of inexpensive shampoo that everyone in your family can use. Suave shampoo is a good example. Ask yourself whether you actually need to replace a particular product. If you can do without it, you've just saved a nice piece of change.

Hair Styling

Whatever your thoughts on hair, I'm sure we will all agree that you need to keep it looking good. You can't walk into an interview with shaggy and unkempt hair regardless of your gender. Furthermore, mature men and women opt for hair colors and styles that may make us look like we're "more up for the challenge" when competing against younger people for jobs. Therefore we need to spend some money in hair salons and barbershops.

I'm going to address this topic from the viewpoint of this book, which is to save money. Some of you won't like what I have to say, and that's okay if you disagree and choose to ignore this section. I won't be offended. But I am going to offer some suggestions in the event you want or need to save.

For many men, professional hair expenses tends to be minimal; a haircut every 4 to 6 weeks, although I know of plenty of men who opt for much more frequent visits to the barbershop. For women, it's typically more involved with cuts, styling, perms, coloring, etc. But I also know some very successful women who make infrequent visits to their favorite salon. If you've read this far, you're interested in saving money for hair services, so here we go.

When: Ladies, you may have established a nice rapport with your stylist. That person may know exactly what you want and when. He or she may also be your confidant. An easy way for some savings is to simply pick less expensive services or styles. Or can you stretch the time between visits. Both suggestions spare you the awkward situation of going to another stylist.

Men, can you stretch the time between your barber visits by a week or two? Have your barber cut your hair shorter so you can go longer between cuts.

Where: For some this may be very difficult, but perhaps you can go to another shop and get the same services for less money. It may mean that you look for a shop is less exclusive areas, or that you might try going to a beauty school. Remember, your unemployment is temporary, and once you find another position you can go back to your preferred shop. For women, this could be a large savings. You might want to get referrals from friends, family, or coworkers. I don't advise getting any kind of professional services by blindly walking into an unknown establishment.

What: Think about each service you have done on your hair on a regular basis and how much it costs. Do you really need it? Talk to your stylist about it; if he or she doesn't want to lose you as a customer, you might get cheaper alternatives or you may find you don't need all of those services.

Who: Can you do some of those same services yourself? Men, if you find yourself with a hairline that has recede to the back of your head, can you buy a set of $25 hair clippers and do it yourself? And ladies, drugstores have aisles of colors and perms. When I was a kid, my mother and my aunt would swap off and give each other perms and hair color treatments. If you have a friend who would be willing to help you, make it more fun with a glass of wine and music. And guys, the hair color aisles usually have a section for men, and with most of these products you can do it yourself.

Ladies, take care of your own nails. Manicures and pedicures fall under the luxury category and should be off limits for the duration of your unemployment.

How: The easiest way to trim hair related expenses is to get rid of the hair. Ladies, before you start cursing or wishing me dead, this is more directed at men. I have friends of all ages who simply shave their heads. New people you meet, such as prospective employers, won't know you recently shaved your head and it looks perfectly normal and acceptable. Your friends and family will get over the change soon enough because you'll still be the same fun and caring guy you've always been.

Ladies, if you're motivated to save money, then look into completely new styles that are easy to maintain yourself but still flattering. Besides, it may be time to give up that bouffant style anyway. Only kidding...

Hair Styling on the Tiers:

Moderate

Talk to your barber or stylist for less expensive alternatives. Stretch the time between visits. These suggestions will save you money and are the least difficult.

Motivated

From referrals, find another barber or stylist who will provide the same services you currently get but for less money. You may have to go to a less exclusive area to do this. If available, consider going to a beauty school. Eliminate those services you don't need.

Extreme

Do some or all of your hair styling and or cutting yourself, or have a friend help you. Men, shave your head; ladies, pick a style you can maintain yourself.

Clothing

If you'll be looking for a job where you know you absolutely won't need to wear a business suit for interviews, then you've spared yourself a headache and a major expense. You also saved yourself some time as you can probably skip this section. Chances are, though, you're interested in getting some ideas for additional savings on clothing in general, so please read on.

You need to maintain a professional image no matter what job you had or what type of job you're searching for. Dressing up for interviews is a must. If your last job was in a professional environment then you're probably all set with at least one business suit and appropriate shoes. Chances are that outfit is recent enough and it will suffice for the interviews.

However, these days, most of us do not have to wear suits on a day-to-day basis. Ladies, perhaps the last time you wore a suit was on the interview for your last job, and for men it was most likely for a relative's wedding or funeral. Regardless, take a look at what you have and try it on. If you think that it will be sufficient and you don't look like you stepped out of a time warp, then have it dry cleaned or pressed. Like the rest of us, it may have shrunk while it was hanging there unused in the closet (wink wink), so have it altered. Alterations are far less expensive than a new suit.

Most people can use their business suits for a number of years, but even though they tend not to be trendy, eventually they do look out of date. Get a second opinion from someone you trust as to whether your business outfit is still current. You'll have enough competition for your next job; don't add the extra obstacle of a disco era outfit.

So where do you go for that new suit, your nearest department store? NO! Not unless they are having at minimum a 40% off sale. These places sell the latest styles at top dollar. Yes, the clothing is of better quality and you'll look like a million dollars, only you don't have a million dollars. Look for other places to make yourself look just as great.

Seek out the clothing discount centers. You know, these are the ones that have words like warehouse or factory as part of their names. The selection in these stores is huge and so are the savings. Plus the salespeople in these stores are usually more knowledgeable and helpful than discount department stores.

Deeper discounts on suits can be found at super discount stores like TJ Maxx or Marshalls. The selection won't be the best and don't even bother to look for help. But if you look hard enough, you may find something that will fit you. The prices will be a fraction of what you'd pay at a department store, so even if you have to take your suit to a tailor or seamstress, your savings will still be significant.

Here's a trick if you're buying a new outfit. Some retailers will offer an additional 10% off the already reduced price if you are willing to open a charge account. This could save you another $20 to $40, BUT, here are some caveats: You may not qualify because you're unemployed. And remember charge accounts balances accrue interest. You'll realize your savings only if you pay off the entire account balance within the 30-day cycle, otherwise your savings will quickly be offset by interest or finance charges.

For those who are truly frugal, thrift shops may be an alternative. As much as I have been thrifty in the past, I can honestly say that I've given clothing to charity shops with the price tags still on them. And I have been in these shops from time to time and have seen merchandise that's clearly never been worn. If you have a very tight budget and need decent clothing to interview, there is absolutely no shame in checking out these places. Chances are slim that you'll find that perfect suit in exactly your size, but if you can find one that is reasonably close, dry cleaners, tailors, and seamstresses can work wonders. The other person at the interview table will have no inkling on the history of your new suit. Incidentally, I would not advise buying used shoes; go to a discount shoe seller instead.

Consignment shops are another alternative for women. Many will take only clothes from certain designers or brands that have been purchased recently. Clothing is not donated to these shops, but rather sold on consignment for a fraction of the original price. That means the former owner gets a percentage of the sale price. Look for better consignment shops, where women often discard their clothes after one season. So, not only this is a good way to get great bargains for nicer clothing, but it may be a way for you to generate money for items you no longer wear.

If you are lucky enough to have a friend or family member who is the same size as you, and they are willing to help you out, then you can always borrow a suit. Not everyone feels comfortable loaning their clothes or, worse yet, asking to borrow some. But, if you've got a good close relationship or friendship, this may be another option. Remember, it's all about making the money you have last longer. Pride can be costly; swallowing it is free.

For the rest of your wardrobe, don't buy anything else. Use what you already have. The only exception may be to have a couple of outfits, other than your business suit, that you can wear to networking events or to social events that offer the potential of employment.

Clothing on the Tiers:

Moderate

Look for deep sales at department stores, such as 40% or more on closeout items or end-of-season sales. If possible, open a charge account at the time of sale to get an additional 10% off, but remember to pay the balance in full when the bill comes; otherwise you'll lose your savings to interest.

Motivated

If you need a business outfit, try clothing discount stores if they are reasonably close by. Some of these include Burlington Coat Factory and Gentlemen's Warehouse to name a couple. If time permits, also check TJ Maxx or Marshall's, but these will require alterations to be done with a tailor or seamstress, so consider that additional cost on top of the selling price.

Extreme

Check out thrift shops such as Goodwill, Salvation Army, or other second hand stores. With some dry cleaning and alterations, these suits can look just as good as the other candidates', and no one has to know where they came from. Borrowing a suit may be a longshot, but if you feel comfortable asking, then do so. This is by far the cheapest alternative.

MORTGAGE AND RENT

After food and clothing, shelter rounds out the top three basic human needs. Although our ancestors might have had the advantage of free housing in caves or self-constructed mud huts, today we have to pay for our shelter, and for most of us, it may be the biggest expense we have. Most town or city building codes won't allow mud huts or other forms of primitive housing, so we have to go with conventional housing in the form of a house, condo, or apartment and pay the price.

Home Ownership

Being free and clear of a mortgage is a wonderful thing. The only things you have to worry about are taxes and insurance. However both of those expenses are significant, so please do read on about taxes, and don't forget the discussion on insurance later in this section.

Mortgages: For the rest of us who face that monthly mortgage payment, on the surface it doesn't appear that we have much choice. Unlike other areas where there are multiple ways to save, each month we are faced with a set amount that we are obligated to pay. However there may be more flexibility on the mortgage than you know.

First of all, making your mortgage payment on time can save you money. Most mortgage companies will charge you up to $50.00 extra for a "late charge." Paying a late charge is like throwing money away, so plan your money to insure the mortgage gets paid on time.

Paying extra on the principal each month is a wise idea because it can save you thousands of dollars in interest and can shorten the length of the mortgage by years. But when you're unemployed, this may not be the best use of your cash because you may need it for something else down the road. During you unemployment period, pay only what you need.

Your home is probably your biggest asset, so it's worth the hassle to try to keep it; at least up to a point. If you're having trouble making the monthly mortgage payment, the worse thing to do is nothing and skip payments. That will put you automatically into default and will start the foreclosure process. This may be a good time to look at your loan agreement and carefully read the section on default of payment. It should state exactly what will trigger a default situation and what happens after that.

If you took your mortgage from a friend or family member, you might want to pick up the phone and talk with the lender to see if they are willing to temporarily change the terms of the mortgage. It's worth asking. Should your lender be willing to make a some temporary arrangement, make sure it's in writing and both you and the lender sign it.

If your mortgage was obtained through a mortgage company or local bank it's probably been sold to some other large bank. Your chances of getting someone sympathetic who is willing to help you may be slim, but it's worth the phone call. Banks prefer not to be in the real estate business and foreclosing on homes is very costly and time consuming for the banks. Some might be more willing to work with you than others.

You might consider talking with a professional who specializes in loan modifications. Be extremely careful; there are many companies and individuals out there who are looking for nothing better than to simply take your money and do nothing for you; worse yet, they end up owning your home and throwing you (and your family) out into the streets. You should not have to pay anything up front for these services. Make sure you do your research on this individual or company before you sign anything, and CAREFULLY READ everything. If you don't understand, don't sign, have someone you trust there who can explain all parts of the contracts.

Loan modifications can end up costing you a considerable amount. You may not have to pay anything up front, but the charges may end up being bundled into the new mortgage. Even though you get a lower monthly mortgage payment, you may end up with a longer term mortgage which could mean thousands of dollars more in finance charges down the road. Loan modifications then, have serious future repercussions and should only be done after careful consideration. I would recommend cutting back in many other areas and trying your hardest to stick with the terms of the original loan agreement. Also consider the cost of loan modifications verses the monthly savings; sometimes it may not be worth the effort

You might consider selling your home if 1) you want a smaller and less expensive one; 2) you're moving to another location; or 3) you decide that you no longer want your home. Selling your home because you can't afford it should only be done as a last resort, because in a down economy you'll be losing money. Most likely you paid more for it than it's currently worth, and certainly your home's value will increase once we're in a better economy. And if you owe more than what your home is currently worth, then you're upside down or underwater in terms of your mortgage. Selling at this point would be considered a short sale. If you are forced to sell, seek professional help such as a tax attorney or a financial counselor in addition to a real estate agent who specializes in your situation. Short sales may affect your credit rating and chances of buying another house in the future.

You may have heard the term strategic default, which is only a way to make a bad situation sound acceptable. Although many have done it, walking away from a home and a mortgage is not a good idea. Such actions will destroy your credit. Without good credit, it will even be difficult to find a decent apartment, and buying another home in the future will be nearly impossible.

By all means try to preserve your home. If it means cutting other things, such as cable TV, phone, and even the amount you spend on food and clothing, then do so.

Real Estate Taxes: Real estate taxes are a fact of life. Municipalities do not take failure to pay your taxes lightly; and in the end they can legally evict you and sell your property. But there are a couple of money saving measures you can take that are perfectly legal.

First is early payment. Some taxing authorities actually offer discounts for early payment. For example, in Florida, tax notices are mailed by November 1 and are due by March 31. A 4% discount is available if the taxes are paid by November 30, and a discount of 3% can be taken if the taxes are paid by December 31. The discount drops to 2% for taxes paid by January 31, and 1% if paid by the end of February. No discount is afforded if the taxes are paid in March. On a $5,000 tax bill, 4% equates to $200. Check with your municipality to see if such discounts are available, and if so, plan accordingly.

Second, check with your taxing authority for any exemptions you may take. Again in Florida, there is a Homestead Exemption that reduces the taxable value by $25,000 if the home is the primary resident of the owner. Other exemptions apply to widows and widowers, veterans, disabled citizens, and senior citizens. These exemptions are not automatic and residents must apply for them, so check to see if you qualify.

Finally, it is possible to appeal your tax bill by presenting your arguments to a value adjustment board (VAB). The board is typically composed of city employees and some independent members such as real estate appraisers or real estate agents. You would be more apt to win your case if you present hard and concrete evidence, such as an inequity between what you paid and what your neighbor paid, assuming both houses are of similar design, style, age, and have the same amenities such as garages, pools, lot size, etc. A VAB hearing is not the place to merely complain that your taxes are too high, nor is it the right venue to state your inability to pay your taxes. If you go before a VAB, be prepared with the facts, present them logically and calmly. It's your opportunity to get your taxes lowered, so don't diminish your chances with tears or anger.

Escrow: For those of us with a conventional mortgage, a portion of the monthly mortgage payment goes into an escrow account which covers homeowner's insurance and real estate taxes. Banks and mortgage companies do this to protect their investment in your home because they don't trust us to pay insurance and taxes – not as a favor to us.

My experience with escrow accounts is mixed. In theory, your real estate taxes and insurance policies will be paid automatically; you don't have to do a thing. Also the most fundamental aspect of budgeting is in place because you are, in effect, setting aside money each month for those bills, and when they come due the money is there. What a wonderful process. In reality, there can be problems with escrow accounts.

Most mortgage company escrow accounts will pay real estate taxes in accordance with early payment discounts. Mistakes are more likely to be made with insurance. In my case, flood insurance policies lapsed. I also noticed that the bank paid the wrong insurer when policies were changed. Another common problem is that the amount they charge for the escrow tends to be miscalculated which leads to negative escrow balances. Banks hate lending money for free and will quickly want to make up that negative balance by charging you much more on your monthly mortgage payment. This can lead to surprise increases in your mortgage payment.

The key is to monitor what the bank or mortgage company is doing with your escrow account. By law, they must disclose all disbursements they make on your behalf. Usually it's right on the monthly statement, and most will even send you a yearly recap of the escrow account. Look at this carefully, and make sure that payments are made on time. I know that my taxes are to be paid in November, homeowner's and windstorm policies are paid in June, and my flood policy comes due in August. During those months, I look at my escrow account online to make sure those are paid on time, especially the taxes, because I want to take advantage of the early payment discount.

Another thing to watch on your escrow is how the mortgage company or bank handles the proposed or budgeted payments. There is no way that a bank with thousands of mortgages will know exactly what each customer will pay for insurance and taxes, but you have a better idea. For example, in South Florida we typically have to buy a yearly homeowner's policy, a windstorm policy, and a flood policy. Just scanning the news headlines gives us plenty of indication that insurance carriers and providers are planning premium hikes and by how much. You should also stay informed of what's going on in your community such as proposed tax hikes or special assessments. With this knowledge, you can estimate your taxes and insurance premiums better than the mortgage company.

For example, let's assume homeowner's insurance rates are going up 10% (not unusual for Florida) over the $2,000 charged in the previous year, and the $4,000 taxes are expected to increase by 5%. Assuming both are due in 10 months and there has been no change in the amount the bank charges for the escrow, then there may be a shortfall of $400 (10% increase of $2,000 is $200, and 5% increase of $4,000 is also $200) in the escrow account. The following month after payments are made, you may find your mortgage payment amount has been increased by $100 or more because the escrow account has a negative balance. The bank or mortgage company will want its money back as soon as possible, and it doesn't care by how much your mortgage payment may increase. But if you know in 10 months there will be a shortfall, then you can be proactive and send $40 extra each month with the mortgage payment. Just make sure you clearly mark on the statement (or on the website) that the extra is going towards the escrow account. That way you won't get socked with a large mortgage increase 11 months later.

Condominium and Homeowner's Association Fees: These are fees charged to the condo or property owner for upkeep of common area elements, such as a community pool, a clubhouse, and security, etc. Condo fees usually include a prorated insurance amount (based on a percentage of the unit size to the total living space of the complex) to cover the building in case of loss. The owner usually pays these fees monthly or quarterly, and typically these are not included in the mortgage escrow. In most areas, failure to pay the homeowner's association and condo fees can result in a lien on the property, and even foreclosure. You have to pay these fees. You can't ignore them.

If you are having difficulty paying these fees, talk to your board members. On some rare occasions, if may be possible to temporarily reduce the monthly or quarterly amount if you promise to pay the shortfall in the future. It's worth asking. Use judgment; some boards tend to be sticklers, and some board members enjoy being hardnosed.

Homeownership on the Tiers:

Moderate

Making your mortgage payment on time will avoid expensive late fees. If applicable, take advantage of the early payment discounts for real estate taxes. Check to see if you qualify for any property tax exemptions. Monitor your escrow account and send extra on a monthly basis to cover potential shortfalls.

Motivated

Talk with a qualified attorney or financial counselor to see if you can benefit from a loan modification. Do your research and homework to see if you can appeal your tax rate to your local value adjustment board. If you have mandatory homeowner's association or condo fees, talk with board members to find out whether it is possible to get a temporary reduction.

Extreme

If you are considering foreclosure or short selling your home, seek bona fide professional help, and discuss the ramifications of those actions to your future credit.

Renting

There are many advantages to renting your home over owning it. Usually all maintenance and insurance is the landlord's headache. You have much more flexibility when it comes to moving; typically a 30-day notice is all that's needed when you near the end of the lease, as opposed to trying to sell a house. And often the monthly rent is less than what a homeowner has to pay. The flip side is that you don't build any equity when you rent, but frugal people will invest their monthly savings over homeownership and come out just as well.

Regardless of your views on renting, when you're unemployed, you still have to pay the rent each month. If you don't, you're apt to find your belongings on the curb, and in some states, it only takes a few months of non-payment for that to happen.

There are numerous forms of renting; some rent houses, some rent apartments in rental complexes, others rent condo units, while others may be renting a small studio over a garage. It's impossible for me to account for every type of rental. However I can break it down into a couple of categories: rentals from corporations and rentals from individual investors. I break rentals into these categories because one might give you a break in the rent over the other.

All landlords are happiest when all their units are rented because that means money is coming in. Corporations that own large rental complexes always expect a certain percentage of apartments to be vacant at any particular time; it's considered a cost of doing business. Individual investors own fewer units for rent, and usually feel the pinch of a vacant unit much more strongly than corporations. For example, a person buys a fourplex as an investment and takes on a mortgage in the process. One vacancy means that he's only receiving 75% of his income, but he's got to pay 100% of his mortgage, plus other expenses associated with the building. He will also have significant expenses to get the unit rented out. Therefore it's important that he keep tenants in all four units.

So how does this relate to you? Simple: If you've been a good tenant and paid your rent on time, an individual landlord may be more willing to work with you, especially if you have been living there for more than a year. This may not always work out, but it's worth having a conversation with your landlord. You might also want to sweeten the deal by providing a service such as helping to maintain the property. Whatever is agreed on should be in writing to avoid misunderstandings and potential legal problems.

Does this mean those of you who are living in a large apartment complex have no recourse. No, not at all. Although less likely than smaller investors, rental corporations may be willing to work with tenants, particularly if you've been living there for a long time and have a good record (always paid the rent on time, no complaints, etc.) You may have to make an appointment to speak with the property manager as a starting point. Although your apartment is your home, the complex is a business, and in business there is no such thing as emotions or feelings. Be prepared to hear cut and dried answers and keep your emotions in check. Anger, protests, and tears will have little effect, and may actually work against you. Also be prepared with documentation to prove your financial condition, such as proof of unemployment, bank statements, and any other supporting papers. There is no guarantee you'll get a temporary rent reduction, but it's worth asking the question. Even if you only get a $50 per month rent reduction, take it, because you know that will help you pay some other bill.

Another option you have as a renter is to move. There is a little thing called a lease, however, and that may be a problem. If you are near the end of the lease, then you have more flexibility because now you can either renew or look elsewhere for cheaper rent. Make sure you look at the terms of the lease because you may be required to give a 30-day notice indicating your desire not to renew. If your lease is not near the end, you'll have to look at your agreement to see what it would cost you to break the lease. Remember, a lease is an enforceable contract and you are legally responsible to fulfill your side of the deal.

Moving is a hassle and a major expense. If you are moving because you found a place with cheaper rent, then make sure you're not going to put yourself in a position of actually paying out more. Total your moving costs: movers or truck rental, connection charges for utilities, and security deposit difference. Divide these costs by 12, and add that to the new rent you'll be paying. If it comes out higher than the old rent, then making the move is not worth it. For example, if you found a new apartment for $650 per month and your old place is $700 per month. Over the course of the year lease, this would give you're a savings of $600 ($50 per month times 12). Your new security deposit is $800, but you'll get back $700 from your old security deposit, which means $100 difference. The moving company will charge $1,000 to move your belongings. Cable and phone reconnection charges are another $150, and the estimated miscellaneous moving expenses come to $50. Your total moving expenses are $1,300. Divided by 12 for a monthly breakdown over the first year of your new lease is $108.33. So this move would not save you any money; it would cost you $58.33 more per month ($108.33 minus your $50 per month "savings.") Your choices are to either find another apartment with a monthly rent of less than $591.67 (this is your breakeven point; $700 - $108.33) or lower your moving expenses to under $600.

If a rent reduction or moving still won't ease the financial squeeze, then you may have to look for some other form of renting. Possible alternatives would be moving in with friends or family, looking for roommate arrangements, or even checking into the possibility of caretaker positions where housing is part of the compensation. Obviously, if you're single, then this will be much easier than doing this with a family. These alternatives may be far less than ideal, but remember it is only temporary until you find better employment.

Renting on the Tiers:

Moderate
Depending on the relationship you may have with the landlord or property manager, you could calmly ask for a temporary rent reduction. If you're dealing with a property manager, have documentation in hand to prove your status. It may not work, but it's worth asking.

Motivated
Moving to a less expensive apartment may be an option. Consider the costs associated with moving, including the cost of breaking a lease if applicable. If the total moving costs don't justify the savings, this is not a good option.

Extreme
Temporarily give up your own place and move in with friends or family, or look into renting a room. You may still have to pay something, but it should be a huge savings.

INSURANCE

As much as we all love to hate insurance companies, their purpose is to minimize our risk of loss. The agreement between the insurer and the insured is a policy. It's possible to insure our property, assets, and even our health and lives. The amount paid for coverage is called the premium.

There has been much discussion on insurance in the past few years. Those who live in areas prone to hurricanes or tornados can attest that insurers are pulling out of markets leaving us with lesser known companies or in high-risk pools with high-priced premiums. Health insurance and their providers have also come into the limelight with changes coming soon. State laws also affect the availability of insurance and even the number of insurers. However, the intent of this section is to discuss options to obtain or maintain insurance coverage and how you may minimize your premiums; the politics are purposely left out.

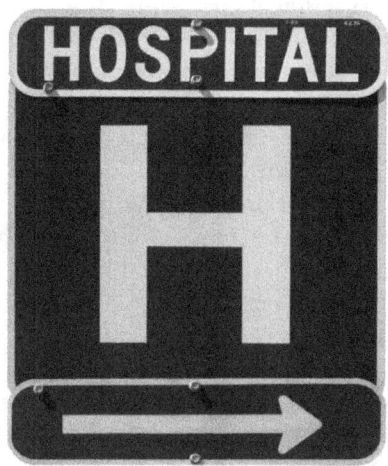

Health Insurance

Health insurance is on a lot of people's minds, and it should be on yours as well. This covers hospital and emergency room visits, doctor's appointments, diagnostic procedures such as X-rays and blood tests, outpatient procedures, and medicines. If you've been ill or hurt recently, you know how expensive all of these things are. We've all heard the $10 aspirin stories, and we know there's some truth in it.

The best way to protect yourself against costly medical bills is by obtaining, or retaining insurance. Unfortunately, health insurance is also very expensive. In spite of the high cost, I do not advocate dropping health insurance – the risk is too high. An overnight hospital stay can easily exceed $10,000, plus you'll get bills from radiologists, labs, and other providers who may have had some input in your treatment. You are responsible for payment of these services, and at these high rates, the expense ramifications could last for years. Nonpayment could result in lawsuits against you and liens against your property, plus it could ruin your credit. This section will give you options to keep your health coverage more affordable.

COBRA: COBRA stands for Consolidated Omnibus Budget Reconciliation Act which was a law passed by Congress in 1985. Part of this law provides health insurance upon termination of employment under certain conditions. Usually, being laid off qualifies the former employee for COBRA coverage. If healthcare coverage was a benefit, the employer paid most of the premium with the balance paid by the employee. The former employee is entitled to the same medical coverage as when he or she was working, only now the former employee must pay the full premium. Coverage usually lasts for up to 18 months after termination.

Employers who offer medical coverage as part of their benefits packages spend a great deal of time seeking the lowest possible premiums at group rates, which means more than one policy. A single policy will tend to be much higher than one at group rates. If you want to keep the same level of coverage upon termination, then applying for COBRA is a good deal. The likelihood of you getting the same coverage with the same deductibles on your own is very slim because you won't qualify for the group rate. However, if you are younger or in good health and you have no pre-existing condition, you may want to think about some other options listed below that may save you some money.

COBRA coverage applies to companies with 20 or more employees. If you were laid off from a smaller company, then there is no federal law governing COBRA for you. However, in some states there is something called Mini COBRA, which works the same way. This one will require you to be more proactive; you'll need to quickly enroll after being terminated because there is a time limit. And it falls upon your shoulders to ask whether your state has such a law. If so, you'll have to apply to the insurance company in writing, and provide payment quickly because the timeframe is very short.

COBRA coverage is a relatively good deal and worth pursuing if you have recently lost your job. If you act upon termination, there should be no lapse in coverage. Most employers will handle the necessary paperwork for COBRA. Mini COBRA requires you to do the work, as I know from firsthand experience. Contact your insurer quickly after your layoff to find out what is needed to enroll.

Spouse's Benefits: If your spouse or partner has insurance through his or her employer, you may qualify for coverage as a family member or domestic partnership. Naturally you'll have to pay the difference for the added coverage, but it might be cheaper than finding a stand-alone policy or even the COBRA coverage for which you might qualify. Keep in mind that many employers only make changes to employee insurance benefits once per year through a period called "open enrollment". You may have to go with the COBRA coverage or some other policy until you can enroll through your spouse's employer.

Groups: Insurers prefer to provide coverage for larger groups rather than single policies or small groups because larger groups are easier and less costly to manage. If you can, look into joining an organization that provides group health plans such as the American Association of Retired Persons, American Automobile Association, professional guilds such as the Freelancers Union or the National Association for the Self-Employed. Most of these organizations have a nominal membership fee and offer wide range of services including health insurance. Look at their websites to get an idea of the types of healthcare coverage they offer.

Online Insurance: There are also websites offering medical insurance such as eHealthInsurance.com as well as others. When dealing with any website for medical coverage, you are on your own. You have no way of knowing what would be in your best interest in terms of coverage and deductibles. You don't even have a guarantee that the insurance you purchased will be accepted by healthcare providers, so be extremely careful. Just because you buy insurance online does not automatically mean that the premium you pay will be less than any other insurance carrier. Be sure to compare policies and premiums from other sources to make sure you are getting a true deal. Always read the small print before you sign up, and make sure you completely understand what you are buying.

Independent Insurance Brokers: From my own experience and research, the best advice may be to seek professional assistance with your insurance needs. The laws are changing rapidly, and unless you're reading up on these changes daily, chances are you won't know enough about the industry to make the best decision. And a mistake in completing the application could result in denied coverage, which would then make it harder to find another insurer. An independent broker could help you make the right decision, help you with the application, and save you money in the process. Make sure the agent is independent, meaning he or she can write policies from multiple insurers. Independent brokers have access to several companies and can find the one that best suits your needs. Brokers who work with a single company will not guarantee your best interests, so make sure you ask.

You shouldn't have to pay for a broker's services because brokers get their income from commissions. It's important however to find a good broker; one you know you can trust. This involves doing some research and asking other people for referrals. Insurance agents, no matter how good, can't set the premiums; they just find the best plan for your needs. Brace yourself for sticker shock because health insurance is expensive even with the best rates.

Higher Deductibles: Deductibles represent the amount of money you have to pay before the insurance kicks in. The trend in the last few years has been moving toward higher deductibles to keep the premiums at a lower level. Many insurers offer different deductible levels for a particular policy, some as high as $5,000 to $10,000. If you and your family are in reasonably good health, higher deductibles may be an option for you because that could considerably lower the premium. But be cautioned: A $5,000 deductible means you are responsible for paying that first $5,000. You may have to make arrangements with the healthcare provider to pay off that amount monthly. Also be careful that the deductible is per policy and not per person if you have a family plan. I suggest working with an independent insurance broker before you make any changes to your policies.

IRA Withdrawals: It may be possible to make an IRA withdrawal to cover the costs of healthcare coverage without incurring an early withdrawal penalty. Keep in mind, however, that if the funds come from a traditional IRA, you will likely have to pay taxes on the money you withdraw. Talk to a tax accountant or a financial professional before you do this; you don't want to inadvertently put yourself in an even more negative situation.

Health Insurance on the Tiers:

Moderate

If COBRA or Mini COBRA coverage is an option, then stay with it. Although not necessarily the cheapest, you'll get the same coverage you had at your old job for up to 18 months. If applicable, check to see if you can get coverage through your spouse's employer.

Motivated

Explore organizations that offer healthcare coverage and consider web-based insurance carriers. Shop around, but be careful. Consult with a reputable independent insurance broker for sound advice.

Extreme

If you're in good health, consider opting for high deductibles because typically policies with higher out-of-pocket expenses have lower premiums. I would also recommend consulting a good insurance broker for this tier as well. Look into the possibility of paying for health insurance by making an IRA withdrawal.

Homeowner's/Renter's Insurance

For most of us, our homes are our biggest investment, so it's worth protecting it from damages resulting from fire or storms, or from liability. Even if you don't own your home, you still want to protect the contents.

If you've got a mortgage, chances are that you are obligated to buy homeowner's insurance. Most mortgage holders will place a portion of your monthly mortgage payment into an escrow account to cover the insurance premium when it comes due. However, it is up to you to find that insurance coverage. In such an arrangement, do not let a lapse in coverage occur because the mortgage holder will find a replacement insurance policy that will probably not be in your best interest, and you'll be stuck paying an astronomical premium. Mistakes can happen, so make sure you monitor your monthly statements for escrow activity regarding your insurance.

In many parts of the country it may be necessary to buy additional policies for large-scale destruction, such as wind (hurricanes), tornados, earthquakes, and flooding. If you are lucky enough to find multiple providers for a specific type of insurance, you can compare premiums and pick the better deal. However, for most of these, such as flood, there is only one provider and the quoted amount is what you have to pay. Because there is no alternative but to buy the insurance, there is no further discussion on these additional policies. The focus of this section is on regular homeowner's policies.

Current Policy: Usually homeowner policies are issued yearly and often renewed automatically. Unless your insurer decides to drop coverage in your area or state, or you've had too many claims, it's likely that you'll stay with that insurer for a number of years. Ask neighbors, family, friends, coworkers, and even church members what they are paying for homeowner's insurance premiums. The more people you ask, the more you'll know whether your rates are within reason. If you discover that your rates are in the ballpark, stay with your current carrier. It's a hassle changing insurance companies, and switching may cost you money for inspections or expensive insurer mandated modifications such as compliance with newer electrical codes, new roofing, or storm protection.

Shop Around: If you think you can get better value for your money, then by all means shop around, particularly if you have a newer home and you've have few or no claims. The process is fairly easy; look online or in the phone book for independent agents who have access to multiple insurers because they can literally shop for you. Limit your calls to insurance agents to two or three otherwise you'll be getting multiple quotes from the same insurer. There are only so many.

Be forewarned. Laws may have changed and newer conditions may be applied to coverage since the last time you applied. Switching insurers may require inspections that in turn could trigger costly improvements to meet newer building codes or modifications to remove a hazard. Other factors now have an impact on policy pricing that weren't in place in the past such as owning dogs, swimming pools, and even recreational items such as trampolines and golf carts. Make sure you have a good dialog with your insurance agent so that you have no surprises when the policy premium is in your mailbox.

Lower coverage/increase deductibles: If you're looking to save money, you might want to lower your coverage, increase your deductible, or both. I wouldn't recommend lowering your coverage unless it was intentionally higher than necessary. You also may not be able to reduce the coverage if you have a mortgage. Be careful if you are lowering your liability coverage; unfortunately, we live in a litigious society and you don't want to increase your risk of lawsuits just to save a few dollars.

Increasing the deductible could also lower your insurance premium. Again, you have to assess the risk versus the savings. Remember, bad things happen to good people all the time. Only you can make this call. If you are not comfortable with the higher risk, then leave your coverage and deductibles as they stand because there are other ways to save money. Conversely, if you are comfortable with the higher risk, do it.

Renter's or Contents Insurance: If you rent, renter's insurance is a good idea to cover the contents of your home. If you own your condo, this is also the same type of coverage available to you. Condominium associations usually purchase the insurance for the exterior of the building, and unit owners pay for it through monthly or quarterly condo fees. A condo owner should not be obliged to buy any additional coverage beyond that for contents. As for renters, the landlord typically buys insurance for the building, but read your lease carefully because sometimes building insurance is the tenant's responsibility. In either case, should your apartment or rented home be destroyed from fire or other hazard, the cost of replacing your furniture, appliances, clothing, linens, etc. will be covered. And the good news is this coverage tends to be relatively inexpensive.

As with the homeowner's insurance, the same three options are applicable for renters or condo owners. If your rates are in line with the market, renew your existing policy. Otherwise, shop around. You can also lower the coverage or increase the deductibles if you need to save money. You'll want to drop coverage only as a last resort. It would cost a fortune to replace all of your belongings.

Homeowner's Insurance on the Tiers:

Moderate

If your current policy is in effect and the premium is in line with the market, then leave it alone; otherwise you may end up paying more.

Motivated

For owners of newer homes, it may be worth shopping around for a better rate. If you find one, there is no need to wait until the current policy expires. When you cancel the old policy, the unexpired portion will be refunded to you. Just make sure you cancel the old policy when the new one starts to avoid a lapse in coverage.

Extreme

If possible, lower the coverage and/or increase your deductibles. Remember, in doing so you are increasing your level of risk. Act carefully, this is your home.

Auto Insurance

Depending on where you live, the number of drivers, and your driving habits, auto insurance can be a huge expense. Policies are normally written for 6 or 12 months, with many insurers allowing you to make monthly payments. Regardless of whether you pay in full or make monthly payments, there is room for savings. Incidentally, I would recommend paying monthly while you are unemployed. Why tie up your cash?

Most states require basic coverage which is typically liability; this is in the event you cause damage to someone else's vehicle, or worse yet, cause injury. Even if your state or area does not require insurance, I would not recommend going without. Should you hurt someone in an accident, chances are very high that you'll be sued. You need to protect your home and assets, and quite likely, future earnings.

Get Rid of Points: Safe driving clearly has its merits, one of which is a discount on your insurance premiums. If you have points on your license from traffic violations or accidents, look into ways of lowering or erasing these points. For example, in Florida, it is possible to take safe driving classes that will remove points. The savings in the long run certainly offset the cost of the course because points usually remain on your license for several years meaning you won't get safe driver discounts for the duration.

Shop Around: The easiest thing to do is to shop around for a better rate on your current coverage. Find the declarations page to your current policy; it contains all of the information you need to provide another potential insurer. You can even shop on the internet, although use caution with this option. It might be wiser to find insurers or agents on the internet and then call them directly. Speaking with a live person is usually best because they are more apt to tailor a policy specifically for your needs and that will save you money.

There is no reason to wait until the policy is about to renew. You can cancel most policies at any time and you'll be refunded the unused balance. For example, if you purchased a six month policy on January 1, and you cancel on March 31, you should be refunded 50% of your premium if you prepaid the entire amount.

Lower Coverage and/or Deductibles: Discuss with your agent the possibility of lowering your coverage and maybe increasing your deductible. Adjusting the deductible may give you the biggest saving. But remember, should you have an accident, you'll have to spend more money having your vehicle repaired. Before you decide on anything, look at what your savings will be for the year compared to the increase in the deductible. If you feel comfortable with the savings but higher risk, then go ahead.

Removing Coverage: The two most expensive components of an insurance policy are liability and collision. As previously mentioned, liability covers injury or damage to others, and this coverage is usually compulsory. Even if it isn't, don't drop this coverage; you don't want to be sued. The other part is collision, which covers damage to your own vehicle, and this is not usually required by law. However, if you have a new car and you still owe on it, the lender may require collision coverage as part of the loan agreement. If you still owe on your vehicle and it's declared a total loss as the result of an accident, you are still responsible for paying off the remainder of the loan. As a rule of thumb, if you are still making payments on your car, then you should keep the collision coverage. The same applies to leased cars and trucks, by the way.

Inversely, if you have an older car and you own it free and clear, then you have the option of dropping collision coverage. Cars nowadays are designed to last a lot longer than those of previous generations. If your car is paid off, is five or six years old with relatively low mileage, and has been well maintained, you might want to consider keeping the collision coverage. Should your car be destroyed, you will get an insurance check for the actual cash value which you can use to buy a replacement. Otherwise getting another car might be difficult because it's hard to qualify for car loan when you're unemployed.

On the other hand, a car more than 10 years old or with high mileage may not warrant the expense of collision coverage based on its cash value. Look to see what your car is worth on BlueBook.com and then make the decision.

The other component is called comprehensive and covers your vehicle in the event of theft, vandalism, and fire. This part is usually inexpensive when compared to liability and collision and the increased risk probably won't justify the small savings in the event your car is stolen.

Auto Insurance on the Tiers:

Moderate

Points on your license will cost you money for several years, so look into ways of having those removed. Make a few inquiries to other insurance companies or agents to see if you can't find a better deal. Be careful to avoid a lapse in coverage between the old policy and the new one.

Motivated

Discuss adjusting coverage and deductibles with your agent. This probably will save you money, but it will also increase your risk should an accident occur. If you are comfortable with the increased risk, then this option may be for you.

Extreme

Removing collision insurance on older cars can save you a considerable amount. It's certainly not wise to remove this coverage if you still owe on your vehicle however. Keep in mind that should your car be totaled in an accident, you won't get an insurance check to help you buy another one.

RV Insurance

Boats, motorcycles, campers, and the like are recreational vehicles, meaning that you don't need them to survive. Motorcycles might be the exception if you rely on one for your normal transportation, meaning that if you didn't have it, you'd have to walk or use public transportation. These are all fun to have, but when money is tight, these toys can become a burden, and that includes insuring them. As with cars, there are some options to reduce the insurance costs.

Shop Talk: Shop around for better insurance rates. Maybe the policy you bought three years ago that has been automatically renewing may no longer be the best deal. It's worth a few phone calls.

Through your agent, look into reducing the coverage or increasing the deductible. If you're not using these toys very much, the exposure to damage may be less, which can make your increased risk more palatable.

Cold Storage: If you are disciplined, you might be able to drop the insurance while you're out of work. This means you can't use the vehicle unless you take on the whole risk, which I don't advise. So wrap that boat, cover that motorcycle, and park that RV in a secure lot to avoid the temptation of using them. Also be wary; some local ordinances prohibit or restrict storing such vehicles in your yard. You may also encounter state or local laws requiring at least some liability coverage. As with cars, if you still owe on the vehicle, don't drop the insurance. Also keep in mind that these vehicles will not be covered in the event of fire or theft. Check with your agent to see if these might be covered for these risks under another existing policy such as your homeowner's.

Lighten Your Load: If you don't use these vehicles much, then why have them at all? This is not the time in your life to shell out money on toys just in case you want to use them. Sell them. Not only will you save a bundle on insurance, you'll also get rid of storage, dock, and maintenance expenses.

RV Insurance on the Tiers:

Moderate

Shop around for better rates on premiums. Call your agent to discuss lowering coverage or increasing deductibles.

Motivated

If you legally can, consider not insuring these vehicles. However while they are uninsured, be sure not to use them and that they are safely secured. Remember, you take on all risk of loss without insurance.

Extreme

Sell or donate your toys if you're not using them. There is no point in paying insurance on unused status symbols.

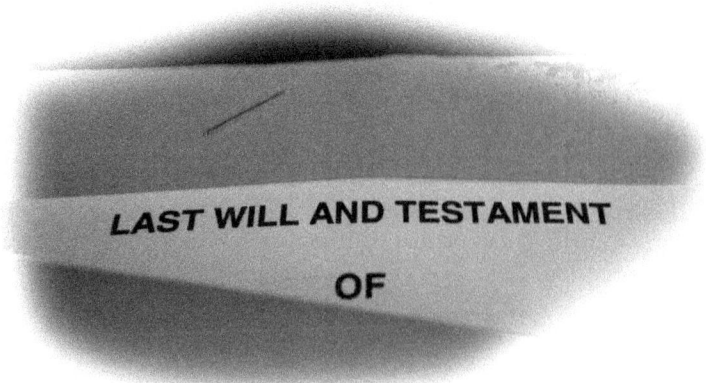

Life Insurance

People have vastly different opinions on life insurance. As the primary breadwinner, some want to protect their spouse and children in the event of unexpected death. In this light, policies with high benefits are purchased to cover the outstanding mortgage or to provide a nest egg that will keep the rest of the family afloat. People without young children may opt to buy smaller policies to cover funeral expenses only. And finally there are those who either have estates to keep the family funded and cover funeral expenses, or those who simply don't care.

Life insurance policies are usually purchased over the long run and the monthly payment is typically a set amount. Sometimes though, the premium increases incrementally as specified in the policy. The only time to shop around is when you initially buy the policy.

Ideally, your unemployment status is a temporary condition in relation to the duration of the policy. If you can afford to pay the premium, then continue to do so. Unfortunately, we usually don't know how long we will be without a job. To that end, there are only two options when it comes to life insurance: Terminate the policy and take the cash value (whole life only – there isn't a cash value with a term policy), or continue paying it. If you decide to cancel and buy a new one after you resume working, remember that a new policy probably will cost you more than the previous one because you will be older. Life insurance becomes more expensive as we age. Furthermore, canceling the policy to take the cash value is usually not a wise investment because you've probably paid much more than the cash value. Really, canceling a life insurance policy should only be a last resort.

Should you need an infusion of cash, it may be possible to take a loan against the cash value of the policy. Talk to your insurance agent or call the insurer directly to see if this is a possibility. Usually this is only available with "whole life" or "permanent" life insurance policies.

There are few options when it comes to life insurance; either you have it or you don't. The motivation to buy the product is driven by family needs, personal preference, and even indifference. So for these reasons, I decided against putting life insurance on the tiers; doing that would be of little use.

HEALTH

Health is a two-pronged issue regarding money: As we all know, health care in this country is hugely expensive. And maintaining good health is critical to generating income. If you're sick or hurt, you diminish your chances of getting back to work, and in doing so you can incur a huge debt. If you are lucky enough to be in tip-top shape, make sure you stay that way. If you are like the vast majority of us and have a medical condition or health issues, then do your best to keep those under control.

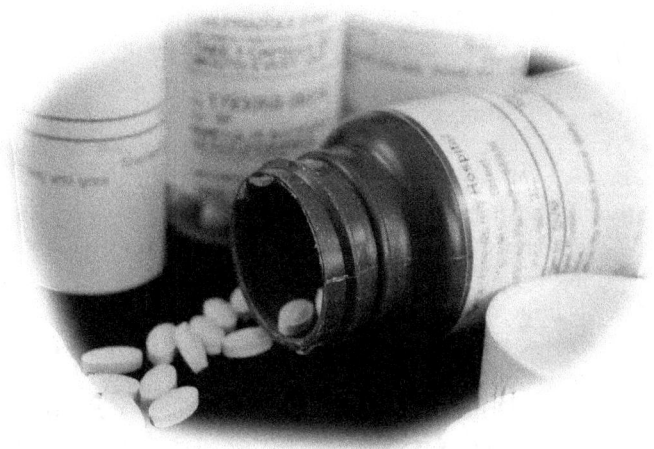

Prescriptions

Prescribed medications are vital because they allow us to work and maintain some sense of a normal life. Without them, we would be in pain, we would have serious crippling disabilities, or worse yet, we could die. Some prescriptions are for the short term and others are for life. Regardless, if our doctors prescribe medications, it's because we need them. Unfortunately, many of these can be very expensive. Yet it is possible to save money and continue using our much needed prescriptions.

If at all possible, discuss using generic medications with your doctor. They may be a good option for your ailment. In spite of reports, generic drugs may not be the exact formula of the brand product. Nonetheless, generics are available for many drugs at a fraction of the cost. Even if you do have prescription coverage, your co-pay will typically be much less if you use a generic drug.

Many insurance companies negotiate with drug manufacturers and work out pricing structures for prescriptions. The result is that the insurance company will have a "preferred" brand over another. For example, for years I have been using a generic drug. The last time I had my prescription refilled, the price almost doubled. I talked with the insurance company and I also discussed it with my pharmacist who was nice enough to call the insurance company on my behalf. As it turned out, the non-generic version ended up being the less expensive alternative! The insurance company had apparently negotiated a better deal with the drug company, resulting in the brand name being less expensive than the generic. Although this may not happen all the time, it is certainly worth the call to you insurance company to find out what the cheapest alternative may be for each of your prescriptions.

As much as possible, look into online pharmacies to fill your prescriptions. There are many out there, including those that also have retail stores. Your savings can be worth the effort, particularly if you buy 90-day supplies.

Many drugstores and pharmacies offer store discount programs. Walgreen's, CVS, K-Mart, Wal-Mart, Target, and even Costco all offer such programs. Typically these programs focus on a list of generic versions of common prescriptions, but some may also include over the counter medications. The benefit of enrolling in such a program is that you can get some prescriptions for as low as $4 or $5. Some do charge an annual fee: $15 to $20 for an individual is not uncommon, and for families, it can be as high as $50. Be forewarned; with some programs you may not be eligible if you already have prescription coverage.

A smart person will be armed with a list of all prescriptions (with the dosage and quantity) and present a copy of this list at three or four pharmacies with such programs. Using this list, get the prices of all your medications, and don't forget to ask if there is an annual fee. To properly compare plans, you should annualize your costs. For monthly prescriptions, multiply by 12, weekly ones by 52, bi-monthly by 6, etc. Then add the annual costs of your covered prescriptions with those that are NOT covered (full price), plus the annual fee. Do this for each plan. The cheapest one wins.

Finally, don't be afraid to ask questions to your doctor. Many times doctors will prescribe one brand over another based on medical literature, the persuasiveness of the drug representative, or even their own preference. But if you ask if there are alternatives to a certain prescription, he or she may be willing to help you determine the least costly one.

If you are currently taking expensive prescription drugs, you might also ask your doctor if you can reduce the frequency consumption. For example, rather than four times per day, is it possible to have the same results with two or three times per day? Be wise and do NOT change your medications, schedule, or dosage without first consulting your doctor.

You might also want to ask your doctor to double the strength if you are willing to cut the pills in half. For example, 50 mg tablets of Drug A costs $100 for 30-day supply, and the same drug at 25 mg costs $90 for 30 days. This means cutting the 50 mg tablets in half would last 60 days rather than 30 days. Although at face value the 25mg is cheaper, the 50mg size lasts twice as long. To see your savings, you need to annualize both: 25mg at $90 per month times 12 is $1,080; 50mg at $100 every other month is $600 per year. $1,080 less $600 means a savings of $480 per year, or $40 per month. As you can see, it's worth asking.

Prescriptions on the Tiers:

Moderate
Use generic drugs as much as possible. Check with your insurance company to make sure you use its preferred drugs.

Motivated
Use online pharmacies to further savings. Find the best prescription discount program for your needs and enroll in it.

Extreme
Find out if you save by purchasing a double dosage pill and cutting it in half. Talk to your doctor about the possibility of reducing the dosage or frequency of medications.

Fitness Centers

The two biggest factors to health can be simply stated as what we put into our bodies, i.e. food, drugs, alcohol, and tobacco, and how we use our bodies through exercise and work. These inputs are discussed in other sections of this book. In this section we'll deal with one of the outputs: Exercise.

Exercise is important in maintaining your weight, mental function and attitude, and overall well-being. Exercise can take on many forms, from regular gym memberships to facilities that offer specialized physical training to simply doing it on your own. Aside from the latter, most programs and facilities require payment.

Many of us join gyms, but a lesser amount actually use them. If you honestly find yourself in that category of paying for a gym but rarely going, then you're wasting money. Ideally, now would be a great opportunity to take advantage of the gym because you have more time, and can go during off-peak hours eliminating crowds and the wait for machines. Plus you can use your trip to the gym as a way to network for that next job.

However, gyms aren't for everybody. Some of us have joined a gym as our New Year's resolution and later found ourselves with fizzled determination. Now we are faced paying $40 to $60 (or more) per month for something we don't use and maybe even just plain hate. Yes, a contract was signed, so we're stuck paying that monthly fee while we're unemployed, right? Maybe not. If you're sure that you won't use the gym, ask the manager to be released from your contract. If not, ask if it's possible to freeze your membership. There may be a small charge to do this, and you may still be responsible for the full term of the membership after you remove the freeze. However, the freeze may free you from your monthly charge while you're out of work. Once you start working, then you can remove the freeze and finish paying the term of your contract.

For those who use the membership but are having problems with the monthly fee, a trip to the manager's office is also a must. There is nothing shameful in saying that you've been laid off – people do understand the involuntary part of it. The gym is no different, and the manager may be willing work with you. See if there are cheaper alternative levels of membership, such as peak hour restrictions, or access to extra programs or facilities, or even a reduced number of visits per week. It's worth asking.

If your gym refuses to help you with your membership fees, you can ask to freeze your membership and find a temporary lower priced alternative. Just make sure you don't take on another full-fledged membership.

Developing your own work out at home is also an option. There are many books to help you devise an exercise program in your home. These include outdoor activity (weather permitting) and exercises to help various muscle groups using very little equipment. This is not a good time to invest in expensive weight or exercise equipment, so make sure you develop exercise routines that use what you already own.

Fitness Centers on the Tiers:

Moderate

If you're paying for a membership, then use it. If gyms are not your thing but you're under a contract, see whether you can freeze your membership during your unemployment.

Motivated

Find out if you can change your membership level for a less expensive one.

Extreme

For those who do want to work out but don't want to pay the monthly fee, then freeze your membership and work out at home.

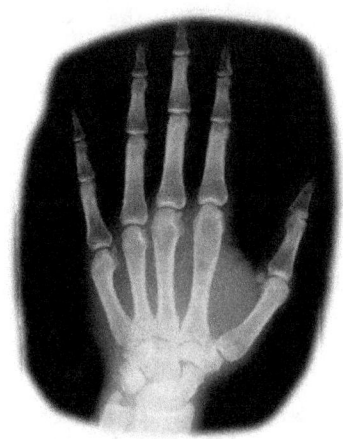

Medical Services and Visits

As much as we try to keep ourselves healthy, things happen. We get sick or we get hurt. Sadly, illnesses and injuries can be quite costly, even with insurance.

If you are insured and you have a manageable deductible, then you're all set. You can seek treatment and not worry. For those who have high deductibles, or no insurance, a serious financial issue may arise. How will your medical services be paid? Ultimately you are responsible.

Where to go: Should you become sick or hurt, use hospital emergency rooms as a last resort because these will result in the highest costs. Before we go any further, let me make myself perfectly clear: If your symptoms include chest pains, shortness of breath, severe pains, or any other life-threatening conditions, then the emergency room is probably the best place for you. And the same holds true if you have suffered a severe injury. Use caution and judgment.

For other illnesses and injuries, try to see your doctor first. An office visit is likely to be the least expensive route. However, be aware of what services your doctor and staff can perform in the office. You want to avoid paying for an office visit only to be referred elsewhere, so when you call to make the appointment, make sure you thoroughly describe your problem.

Urgent care centers are another option because typically these charge far less than emergency rooms. Be careful, some are for profit. Make sure you read all of the paperwork you are given when you arrive.

The system: Insurance companies and medical providers have negotiated prices for all services, from your primary physician to hospitals and medical centers. Healthcare providers can only charge for individual services based on contractual agreements. Then the insurance company may pass a percentage of the contracted amount back to you to pay. That is on top of your deductible. Even if you have insurance, you will incur charges. Depending on the level of your deductible, this can become a significant amount. Additionally, you may receive bills from radiologists, lab companies, physical therapists, etc. for services beyond what your hospital and doctor provide.

If you don't have insurance, there is no contractual arrangement restricting what a healthcare provider can charge. You may end up being charged much more than what your medical providers would expect from an insurance company.

Whopping Bills: If you rack up substantial medical costs because you have no insurance or you have a high deductible, what can you do? The worst thing is to ignore the bills. Once that outstanding amount is in the hands of a collection agency, you're credit has already been affected. You may be hounded by collection agents for years.

Medical billing offices want to close outstanding accounts as soon as possible – and they want cash. Cash in their hands is worth more than future promises of payment. If you've got a sizeable nest egg, you've got a stronger position to negotiate. Some billing offices will settle for less than the total amount; they figure they may as well get what they can rather than have the whole bill sent to a collection agency and never receive a penny. Remember, when you are negotiating it's strictly business. They don't care about you at all. You have to treat the matter without emotions as if you were a paid professional who is managing your money. It's important to start negotiating with these billing offices as soon as you get the bill because the clock will have already started for the billing cycle.

Negotiating and paying off a reduced amount may not be the best option. That will put a huge dent in the funds you need for your unemployment. This is money you'll need to buy groceries, pay the rent or mortgage, utilities, etc.

The best thing to do is to contact the business office for each bill as soon as you get it, and say that you fully intend to pay. Make sure you tell them you are unemployed and that money is tight; but you are willing to make monthly payments. Remain calm, patient, and polite. Become a negotiator and work out a deal you can live with, at least while you are unemployed. Follow up on all of these conversations with a letter to each provider detailing what you have agreed to do, and mail it certified (make sure you keep a copy). This way you will have written proof should they take any further steps against you. Again, let me emphasize that the sooner you act on these bills, the more likely the outcome will be to your advantage. Don't sit on the bills for a month and then call; it'll probably be too late by then, and it doesn't indicate that you truly intend to pay.

Professional Help: If you are not a good negotiator, you can always get professional help, such as an attorney who specializes in these matters, or better yet, a non-profit credit counseling organization. You'll have to pay for their services, but they may be able to negotiate your monthly payments, and may even be able to reduce the total bill. Maybe.

Future Reference: Here is something you can do in case you need medical services in the future. This requires you to be proactive, not reactive, and means you have to do these following things BEFORE you get sick or injured. The onset of a medical emergency is not the time to do research.

Locate charitable clinics, government run hospitals, etc. in your area. Some will provide free services and others may have sliding pay scales where the amount you pay is based on your income. You can find these by doing online searches or looking through the yellow pages of your phone directory. It might even be wise to at least drive by these places in the event you need them. Don't forget to note their business hours. Again, I stress that you should do this before an emergency.

Medical Services and Visits on the Tiers:

Moderate

If you have a high deductible or no insurance, start with your primary physician when you need medical attention, excluding severe medical emergencies. Doctor visits are usually far less expensive than a trip to ER or an urgent care center.

Motivated

Use urgent care centers over emergency room visits, but use judgment on life-threatening emergencies. Quickly negotiate the amount and monthly payment terms after incurring a medical debt.

Extreme

Locate charitable clinics and government-run hospitals in your area BEFORE you need them. Quickly seek help with a non-profit credit counselor for help negotiating medical debt.

VEHICLES

For most of us, cars are essential to get around. Large city dwellers can sometimes get away with being car-free because public transportation is readily available, affordable, and easy to use. But most of us live in smaller cities and towns where public transportation may be somewhat of an ordeal. There's no doubt that we need our cars, and just as much when we're job hunting because employers want people with reliable transportation.

Cars are a major expense, and unless you're buying an antique or some other extremely rare car, vehicles are NOT an investment. As soon as you drive it off the showroom lot, you've already lost value. Plus, cars require maintenance, repairs, and fuel, which further drain your pocketbook. Don't ever believe that cars are an investment.

Car Payments

It's the norm to buy a car on credit; not too many of us can afford to simply write a check for $20,000 to $30,000 for that new car. Most of us take loans for a new (or used) car and pay it off anywhere from two to six years. Typically, we get financing from a company affiliated with the manufacturer, such as Ford Credit or Honda Financing and to a lesser degree, we can get loans from local banks or credit unions.

Having car payments while you're unemployed can be painful. You signed an agreement – really it's a contract – that you will make monthly payments of a set amount. Lenders expect to get those payments regardless of your situation; they don't care whether you are alive and well or at death's door. And they don't care if you are unemployed. So what can you do?

Really, there isn't much you can do except make the payments. If you were savvy by sending additional money each month while you were working, now just send what you are supposed to. Sending extra while you are unemployed will take away from the capital you may need for other things down the road.

If you got your loan from a private individual, such as a family member, see if you can't renegotiate the terms for the duration of your unemployment period. No guarantees that you can, but it might be worth asking.

The same may apply if you talk to your lender, particularly if it is a smaller financial institution such as a local bank or credit union. If you have good credit and have been making your car payments all along, and you've been a good customer (i.e. you've not bounced checks, exceeded your credit limit, etc), it may be worth talking to a customer or loan representative. Smaller banks and credit unions are not in the car sales business, and if they were to repossess your vehicle, they would also be taking a loss. It behooves them to work with you during your time of hardship – and most will. You may succeed in getting new loan terms or you may not. But how else will you find out if you don't talk with them?

For larger lenders, such as GMAC, Ford Credit, or Honda Financing, try the same tactic. The difference is that you may have to make several attempts before finding the right person with the right authority who can make the decision. Another option is to consult a non-profit credit counselor. A good credit counselor may give you the best advice on how to deal with car loans.

If the lender is not willing to work with you, and your car payments prove to be too much each month, there are some options, albeit not great ones. One is to sell the car and payoff the loan, assuming the car is worth more than the outstanding loan amount. This will keep your credit intact, but leave you without a car. If there is another car in the family, then that will also affect your spouse or partner because it means sharing the car. If you live alone, or you are a one-car family, then that means you'll have to rely on public transportation. That may also limit the location of your next job.

If you owe much more than the car is worth, the other option is to allow the lender to repossess the vehicle. Be forewarned that this will all but ruin your credit, and should only be as a last resort. If you think as though this might be your only option, you may want to speak with a credit counselor or the lender before you do anything drastic. Remember, some employers run credit reports on prospective employees, so damaged credit may also hinder your job chances.

Car Payments on the Tiers:

Moderate

Continue making your regular car payments. If you were sending more each month while you were working, send only what is due.

Motivated

If at all possible, see if you can renegotiate the terms of the loan while you are out of work. There may be a small chance that you are able to do this – it's worth exploring.

Extreme

Sell the car with the payments and pay off the loan. This will keep your credit intact. Only as a last resort should you allow the lender to repossess your vehicle.

Maintenance

Cars nowadays are designed to last much longer than those driven by our parents. Advances in technology, and demand for better quality, have resulted in cars that can easily surpass 150,000 miles. Even 200,000 miles is becoming more commonplace. Of course to achieve that kind of mileage vehicles have to be properly maintained.

Maintenance takes on two forms; preventive and repair. Preventive maintenance includes changing the oil, rotating your tires, and tune-ups. Preventive maintenance keeps your car running at peak performance. Repair means replacing broken or worn parts, such as low brakes, worn tires, or any other part of the engine that has failed or is near to doing so. Repair includes fixing or replacing things before they break down, not just after they have.

Ideally, it's better to replace worn parts than to endure a breakdown for several reasons. First, your car may fail in an unsafe neighborhood. Second, a car that suddenly stops running could result in a serious accident. And third, a breakdown can end up costing you much more money because the failure may cause further damage, you may incur towing charges, and you may be at the mercy of an unscrupulous repair shop.

Keeping your car well maintained and in good condition reduces the likelihood of breakdowns, and keeps it safer. Both will also increase the life and value of your car. Unfortunately, keeping your car maintained costs money.

Where-Oh-Where to Go: Taking your car to the service department of a car dealership has its pros and cons. The pros include technicians who are trained specifically for the make of your car. Cars have become very complex and the chances are unlikely that a mechanic knows all the ins and outs of every car brand. Dealerships have mechanics with the latest training, and have resources from the manufacturer on hand. One con here is that service departments at dealerships typically charge more.

Service centers, such as Sears automotive centers, will do most maintenance and repair work, and tend to be less expensive. The flip side is that their mechanics may not have specific training for all makes and models. However, many people are satisfied with the general services that these centers provide.

Although fewer, there are still local garages and auto shops. These tend to offer most services, with the owner many times being the chief (or only) mechanic. Depending on whom you ask, these types of places are either saviors or crooks. The key is finding one who does good work and is honest, which may be tough.

If you think that your current mechanic or service center charges top dollar, then it may be time to switch. Good mechanics are like a good doctor; once you have a good one, then you want to stick with him or her. But when you're watching your money, it may be time to change, even if it's just temporary. Make sure you ask as many people you can for referrals.

So how do you save money and still keep a well maintained vehicle? Well, there are a variety of things you can do. Read on.

What-Oh-What to Do: First of all, use common sense. Although it's important to keep your car in tiptop shape, this may not be the time to make cosmetic repairs. If the defect does not pose a safety hazard, won't impede the performance, and won't cause you to be ticketed by the police, then defer this maintenance.

Read the maintenance section of your car's manual. Yes, I know, nobody reads it and it's probably in the bottom of the glove box, in one of the door pockets, or even in the far back of the trunk. But, you're not working and can afford to take a few minutes to look at it; at least the maintenance schedule. Be smart about what your car needs and what it doesn't need. Gone are the days of the every 3,000 mile oil change. Most newer cars don't need that. So, avoid paying for unnecessary maintenance.

As with several other things, watch for coupons and specials, even with the service center of your choice. If you think that another service center will be a better deal, call your current one before making the switch. They may have a policy to meet competitors' prices, and might even be running savings programs that you may not know about. So put yourself on their mailing list (both U.S. mail and email). For example, I've been taking my car to the same place for years. I had no idea they had a loyalty program where after four oil changes, the fifth one is free. I found out by accident. Fortunately I have a good relationship with my service manager who went back through his records and punched a card so that I will now have two free oil changes. Also ask if your service center will accept competitors' coupons.

If you are lucky enough to have a mechanic you trust and who is knowledgeable about the car you drive, ask him or her to perform only the needed maintenance. At certain mileage points, larger maintenance items, such as replacing the timing belt, are recommended. These recommendations are based on average climates, driving patterns, and usage. The mechanic should tell you if these items are truly needed when you near milestones or if they can be deferred.

What Oh What Did You Say? We've all had the experience where we take our car in for some small repair or maintenance only to be told they found some other larger problem. Your first question should be along the lines of "How much time before it actually breaks?" followed by "How much will it cost to fix it?" Then I would call several friends or family members to find another trustworthy garage or mechanic, make an appointment, and get a second opinion. While you're there, get that second quote. Just as people don't go for major surgery without a second opinion, you shouldn't do the same for your car.

To Do or Not to Do…It Myself: If you are mechanically inclined and have access to at least a driveway, can you do any of the maintenance activity yourself? Clearly, this is not for the average person, including me, although I have done some of these things in the past. Be careful, however, that you don't void your warranty and be aware of any environmental laws pertaining to your actions, such as disposal of used engine oil.

Car Maintenance on the Tiers:

Moderate

Look for coupons and specials for the services you'll soon need. Get on your service center's mailing list for monthly specials. Ask your mechanic if he or she will accept competitor's coupons or match their advertised specials. Defer cosmetic repairs.

Motivated

Find another trustworthy service center or mechanic that charges less. Get his or her opinion for the timing of larger maintenance items. For larger and unexpected mechanical problems, get a second opinion.

Extreme

Do your own maintenance, or have a friend or relative do it for you. Make certain that those doing the work, including yourself, know what they are doing and follow all applicable laws.

Gasoline

Ever since the first oil embargo of 1973, this country has never embraced the fact that we are totally dependent upon foreign oil. Granted, over the years cars have become more fuel efficient, and we now have hybrids that make those precious gallons of gasoline stretch for miles and miles. However, most of us don't have a hybrid; we have plain old engines that burn a hole in our pockets.

Gasoline prices go up and down depending upon some real or perceived problem somewhere on the globe. Once the problem seems to be resolved, the prices will drop some, but not quite to the previous levels. Generally, we pay more at the pumps each time we go. We need to face the reality that we may never again see gasoline selling at 99 cents per gallon.

So, what can we do? The easiest thing we can do is conserve. This can be done two ways: Changing our driving habits and using our cars less frequently.

We've all read and heard various tips and tricks that will save some percentage of gasoline, and if you do them all, by some miracle, the savings percentage adds up to more than 100%. Needless to say, that's impossible. But it is possible to save gasoline by improving the way you drive your car. Here are some ways:

- Drive the speed limit. The faster you drive, the more gasoline it takes, so slow down.
- Use cruise control. This keeps a steady speed and avoids the tendency to speed up suddenly.

- Coast as much as possible. If you see the traffic light changing to red further down the street, take your foot off the gas pedal and simply coast, rather than maintaining your speed and braking at the last minute. Not only will this save gas, but it will also make your brakes last longer.

- Open your windows. Running the A/C puts an extra load on the engine and will reduce your gas mileage. Most experts agree that wind drag will not offset the savings. However, if you're going on a job interview and it's 95 degrees outside, use your A/C; no need to walk into an interview looking like a wet mop.

- Avoid "gunning" your engine. We're all human and get frustrated with other drivers or tedious traffic situations, and we tend to "step on it" to get past the annoyance. Unfortunately, each time we speed up drastically, we are burning extra fuel, which equals money. Ease up on the gas pedal, and get rid of your frustrations by reducing your stress.

We can also conserve gas by changing the timing and frequency of our driving. Here are some more tips:

- Stack your trips. There are certain short trips that you know you do every week or every month. Why not try to "stack" your errands and do them all at once? It takes far less gasoline if you make one trip with two stops rather than two separate trips. It also saves you time.

- Plan your trips. If you are going to do several errands, stop and think about the order you'll do them before you leave. Why drive back and forth across town two or three times when it can be done once?

- Plan your route so that you encounter the fewest stoplights. Idling at red lights does waste fuel. You may not be able to avoid all lights, but whichever ones you can, will help, provided that you didn't drive an extra ten miles.

- Time your trips. One advantage to not working is that you have more flexibility as to when you can do your shopping, errands, etc. Why not do them on off-peak traffic hours, such as mid to late mornings or early afternoons? Everybody knows that being stuck in traffic is unpleasant, but your gas mileage also suffers.

- Bag your trips. There is a way to save 100% of your gasoline: Don't burn it. In other words, you should ask yourself if you really need to make that trip. Each time you back out of your driveway and go someplace, you're burning gasoline, which equates to burning money. If you don't need to make that trip, don't. Or defer it until you need to make another one.

- Keeping your car well maintained also increases your gas mileage. We've all been behind a car that's running poorly and we can smell gasoline in the exhaust; that's just plain wasteful, not to mention bad for the environment and our lungs. A well-maintained engine will use less gas. Also keep your tires at the proper levels; low tires will reduce your gasoline mileage.

All of the above tips can save precious gas, and don't put much of a crimp in your lifestyle. But there are other things you can do as well, although they do mean some change to the normal way you do things. Who knows, some of these changes might actually be fun!

- Walk. Is it possible to walk instead of driving? Only you can answer that, but if it's possible, use foot power rather than your car. Kill two birds with one stone; exercise and save money.
- Bike. This isn't for everybody, but certainly for many this is an option. Enjoy the fresh air and wind as you save your dollars.
- Public transportation. If it's available, try to use it as much as possible instead of driving. It is cheaper than using your car.

Gasoline on the Tiers:

Moderate

Conservation is the easiest way to save on gasoline expense. Change your driving habits to lighten your foot on the gas pedal. Plan your activities so that you make one trip out, use the shortest distance between stops, and make them during off-peak traffic.

Motivated

Keep your car running at peak performance. Defer making unnecessary trips until you need to go someplace.

Extreme

Walk or bike instead of driving whenever possible. Use public transportation as much as you can.

UTILITIES

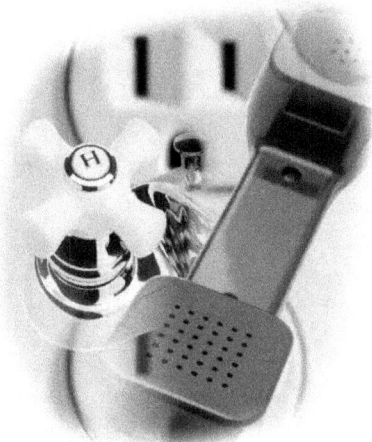

Utilities are conveniences that we all take for granted. We open the faucet and clean water comes out. Flip the switch, and the light comes on. Touch the thermostat and the furnace or AC makes us comfortable. Of course, we have to pay for these, and some are not cheap. Fortunately most of these utilities are billed by usage; the more you use, the more you pay. So the answer lies in using less.

Heating and Cooling

This may be your biggest monthly utility bill, especially during peak seasons. There are many alternatives available to help you reduce your heating and cooling costs, such as replacing old windows with energy efficient ones, adding insulation, and even replacing your old furnace or AC system with a newer and more efficient model. Although these are all proven alternatives, and some with tax savings, they all require a substantial cash outlay, which is not so good when you're trying to preserve your funds.

Unless you have the funds to carry you and your family for more than two years without a job, then don't even consider taking on this expense during your unemployment. Unfortunately, things do break and need replacement; this should be the only exception.

The good news is that there are some cost saving measures for your heating and cooling that require little or no cash outlay. The first is simply being more energy-conscious. We've all heard this; some of us as far back as 1974 with the first energy crisis: Lowering your thermostat for heat and raising it for AC will save you money.

Touch that Dial: There is no doubt that heating, no matter what type of system you have, is expensive. The biggest single way to save is by lowering your thermostat; even a few degrees will result in savings. But if you want to see some significant savings, then adjust your thermostat to 68 degrees during the day and 60 degrees at night. This easy adjustment makes a huge difference in your heating costs, regardless whether you are using electric, gas, or oil. I lived most of my life in New England, so I know what cold winters are, and I'll be the first to admit that 68 degrees is not exactly what I call warm. But to help offset that chill, here are some ideas:

- Run ceiling fans on low speed and on the "winter" setting where the air blows towards the ceiling to recirculate the warmer air back down along the walls.
- Put area rugs on bare floors to reduce that icy feeling on your feet.
- Dress up! Wear long sleeves and long pants, thick socks, cozy slippers, etc. Save your t-shirts, shorts, and flip-flops for the summer.
- Keep yourself warm by using heating pads and electric blankets. It's much cheaper to warm yourself than to heat the whole house.
- Weather proof your home by caulking and sealing cracks around doors and windows.

Inversely, for those who live in areas with long hot summers, cooling your house is just as expensive. Again, the biggest saving measure is to bump up that thermostat to 80 degrees. I now live in South Florida, and I'm quite comfortable at 80, but most of my fellow Floridians find that unacceptable, and keep their homes and offices at icy temperatures that turn my fingers blue. I just find it odd how 68 degrees in the winter is much too cold, but in the summer it's too hot. In any case, below are some ways to help keep you feeling cooler when you maintain your home's temperature at 80 degrees:

- Use ceiling fans on the "summer" setting where the air blows downward to circulate the cooler air near the floor.
- Aim portable fans at yourself.
- Avoid using the oven. When you're not using your computers, TVs and other electronic devices turn them off. Dim or replace halogen lights. All of these things generate heat which makes your cooling system work harder
- Wear lighter and thinner clothes, preferably loose fitting, or just wear less.
- Drink plenty of cold liquids.
- Close drapes and blinds in windows exposed to direct sunlight.
- Sealing cracks around doors and windows will help to keep the heat out.

Replace that Dial: Like everything else nowadays, new thermostats are digital. The good news is that most are programmable, meaning you can set the temperature by the time of day. For example, you can set the temperature for 68 degrees starting at 7:00 am until 8:00 pm, and then for the rest of the time the temperature will be set at 60 degrees. If you are committed to saving money by lowering your heating costs (also works for cooling by the way), then this may be worth a small investment. Programming your thermostat eliminates having to remember to lower the heat at the end of the day. Plus, some of them come with a locking feature that prevents others in your household from "upping" the heat a few degrees while you're away. Most are no more difficult to install than a light switch, and they are well below $100, with a fairly good selection less than $50. Save further by installing it yourself or having a family member do it for you. Having it installed by a HVAC service person probably will cost you another $75 to $100.

Closed Door Policy: For heating and cooling, a common recommendation is to close off or seal off rooms that aren't used. There are two schools of thought with this measure. On the surface it appears to make sense: Heating or cooling 200 square feet less means savings. Well, maybe. Some heating systems are designed to circulate either air or water, and closing off part of that system may result in a less efficient system. Obviously, if your sole heating is a wood stove, then this makes perfect sense, except you need to know if there are any pipes in that section of the house you're not going to heat. Frozen pipes can result in a lot of costly damage.

In warm and humid areas, the air conditioning system removes humidity from the air. Closing off a room can lead to a musty smell and possibly mold. Furthermore, most home cooling systems are designed to circulate the air, and blocking off a part of the house can make the circulation less efficient. In either case, it may be wise to consult with an expert before closing off part of your house.

Energy Audits: Some utility companies offer free audits. If you elect to have this done, a representative will come to your home and inspect your heating and cooling systems. He or she will make suggestions to improve the system performance, identify things you can do to save money on your heating/cooling costs, and may offer programs or services to help you save more. Be careful of that last one. Remember, they represent a company that is interested in making money. You are unemployed and need to save your money. Take advantage of the things that you can do for free or a few dollars, but don't sign up for programs that end up costing you more every month. And certainly don't buy any new equipment unless it's broken. You can participate in these programs when you're back on your feet and are more concerned with long-term savings.

Keep it Purring: Regular maintenance on your heating and cooling systems will also help save money by keeping them running at optimal levels. This applies to not only the furnace or A/C system, but also ducts, filters, and even radiators or baseboard heating elements. Dirty filters reduce the airflow, making the systems work harder. Leaking air ducts are nothing but wasteful; inspect them and use the proper tape (contrary to its name, duct tape is usually not recommended). And vacuum your radiators and baseboards. Removing the layer of dust is like taking a blanket off from your heating elements.

Space, The Final Frontier: Space heaters are another option. When used in addition to your regular heating system, these can keep you warm when you're likely to be in one area of your home for a while, such as when you're watching TV, sitting at the computer, or reading. This will allow you to lower the thermostat to the rest of the house and selectively warm the room you are occupying. Space heaters can also be used in regions with moderate temperatures, even eliminating the need to turn on the furnace.

Space heaters are a relatively inexpensive way to heat a small area. And they are much more efficient than heating the whole house. There are a variety of them out there, such as 1K clear kerosene heaters that pump the heat, and a whole array of electric ones. Some have fans to blow the warm air, and others use radiant heat. Regardless of your preference, I can't urge you strongly enough to use extreme caution. Some are less prone to fires than others, but all can pose some serious risks, include carbon monoxide poisoning. Don't leave any of these heaters unattended, be careful when used around children and pets, and always READ THE MANUALS COMPLETELY AND CAREFULLY before the first use. These manuals are not just covering the manufacturer's butt in case of lawsuits; they contain important safety information to eliminate fire, injuries, and even death. Be warm, but be wise as well.

Look Around: Those who use wood, coal, or oil for heating have a slight advantage over the rest who use either natural gas or electricity. You can shop around for the best prices. Unless you are locked into a contract, a few phone calls before the next delivery could save you considerably.

Some years it seems as though natural gas is the most economical fuel, and in other years oil seems to be the best. In some parts of the country, electricity is the better deal. Regardless, this is not the time to make any capital investment in your home, such as replacing your heating system. Yes, in the long term it will save you money, but remember, right now your focus is conserving your funds for your short-term unemployment period.

System Shut Down: A sure-fire way to save on heating and cooling is by not using it. No one is suggesting you turn off your furnace in January or your A/C system in July. But what about during between seasons like September or April? You know your particular section of the country better than I, but certainly there are times when the weather does moderate. For the largest part of the country, that means spring and autumn. Ask yourself if it's warm enough to turn off the heat when the worst of the winter has gone by, or check if it's actually cool enough outside to open the windows in late September. Whether you believe in global warming or not, weather abnormalities are seem to be more frequent. So, if you get that 60 degree day in January or even that 60 degree day in July, shut the system and open the windows. A single day without your system can save your precious kilowatts or gallons of oil.

Heating and Cooling on the Tiers:

Moderate

For some fuels, such as wood, oil, or coal, look for the best prices before you have to order the next shipment. Turn down your thermostat a few degrees while you are heating, and raise it when you're cooling. Run fans, dress appropriately and take other measures to keep yourself comfortable without taxing your heating and cooling systems.

Motivated

Weatherproof your home by caulking and weather-stripping your doors and windows. Look for free energy audits but be wary of pressure to make you buy products or services. Maintain your heating and cooling system to achieve peak performance, including dusting and vacuuming radiators and baseboard elements. Lower your heating temperature a few extra degrees, and a couple more at night. Inversely, set your air conditioning at a few degrees higher than you normally do.

Extreme

Lower your heating temperature to 68 degrees during the day and 60 degrees at night, and raise your air conditioning temperature to 80 degrees. Turn off your systems in moderate seasons and on nicer days; use your windows to regulate the temperature in your home. Use space heaters as much as possible, especially the ones that put out a lot of heat such as kerosene heaters, but use extreme caution. Get a programmable thermostat, but install it yourself or have a friend do it for you.

Water and Sewer

If you have your own septic system, then there is no monthly charge by your local municipality. As with everything else, take care of your septic system to avoid problems because this is not the time to have your septic tank serviced, or worse yet, replaced.

For the rest who pay for sewer service, there typically isn't much flexibility for savings. You get billed for the service and you have to pay. There usually isn't competition or an alternative for this service.

In either case, the focus in this section will be on water consumption. If you use on your own well, then there is no monthly charge, but you may want to read this section anyway because conserving water is everybody's responsibility.

Most of us are charged by our city, town, or county based on how much we use. The more we use, the more we pay. The good news is that water is still much cheaper than gasoline! But just because it's relatively cheap, it doesn't mean we can't cut back our consumption to lower our monthly or quarterly bills.

The Throne: The single biggest water use in an average home is the toilet. According to the American Water Works Association's website, Drinktap.org, toilet flushing represents 26.7% of your water bill. With this in mind, avoid unnecessary flushing by not using your toilet as a trashcan or a food disposer. This is an easy saver. For the more conscientious saver, here is a rhyme I heard years ago: "If it's yellow, let it mellow. If it's brown, flush it down." We all have our tolerance levels, and this may or may not be for you. Remember, however, each time you flush money goes down the drain.

Laundry Day: According to the same website, the next biggest consumer of water is your washing machine. This comes in at 21.1% of your water bill. No one will argue that we need to wash our clothes, but perhaps we can be wiser about it. For example, small or partial loads are an inefficient use of water. Waiting until there are enough dirty clothes to fill the washer is an easy cost saving measure. Another cost saver is to wear some clothing more than once. Obviously some types of clothing can and should only be worn once before they're ready for the laundry. But if you just wear a pair of jeans to watch TV, those jeans are not dirty; you can wear them again.

On final note on laundry: Cutting down on laundry not only saves water, but also the electricity needed to wash and dry (dryers use a lot of power). Don't forget that power was also used to heat the water.

A Sprinkle a Day: Showering makes up the third-largest water use, which comes in at 16.8% of your water usage. I'm not going to discuss your personal hygiene, but there is plenty of room for savings in regards to showering. Maybe you want to think twice about that second or third shower of the day; do you need it? If so, that's fine; if you're not sure, then skip it. Your skin may actually thank you.

Letting the water run while you shampoo and lather up is a complete waste. Chances are you're also wasting shampoo and soap in the process. Get wet, shut the water while you lather up, and then turn it back on when you're ready to rinse.

There are also inexpensive shower heads or inserts to shower heads that can reduce the water flow but maintain pressure. These are easy to install and are widely available from any hardware store, home and garden center, or even discount department stores.

Other Water Uses: Again according to the American Water Works Association, leaks account for 13.7% of the water usage. A steady drip equates to gallons of water over 24 hours, then continues to become dollars wasted over the billing cycle. Fix all leaks; they're a complete waste otherwise.

Outdoor watering is also a drain. If you need to water your lawn or garden with a hose and a sprinkler, use a kitchen timer to remind you to shut the faucet. Running a forgotten sprinkler for hours is wasteful. Inexpensive timers are available and can attach to your hose in seconds. If your system is automated, as is the case in many parts of the country, then look at your settings. Can you get by with half as much watering time per cycle? Do you need to water every day?

Other savings can be obtained by only running your dishwasher when it's full, installing efficient aerators for your kitchen sink, and thinking twice before letting the water run. Rather than letting the water run for three minutes for it to get cold, keep a pitcher in the refrigerator. You know your home and your habits better than anybody else, and I'm sure you can think of other ways to save on water usage.

There are government programs that offer incentives, such as rebates or tax savings if you install water efficient toilets. Under normal circumstances, it may make sense to participate in these programs, but maybe not when you are unemployed. You should consider saving your cash rather than taking on the expense of replacing plumbing fixtures. You can always make these investments for long-term savings after you're beyond your short term unemployment.

Water Usage on the Tiers:

Moderate

Avoid unnecessary toilet flushing. Wait until you have enough dirty laundry to fill your washer; avoid small and partial loads. The same applies to the dishwasher. While you're in the shower, turn off the water when you're lathering and shampooing. Fix all water leaks.

Motivated

Install water efficient aerators in your sinks, and replace shower heads with those that use less water. Keep showers to a minimum. Consider cutting back on outdoor watering.

Extreme

Consider waiting for multiple uses before flushing. Keep showers to once per day as much as possible. Do some research to find and replace all faucet aerators and shower heads with the most efficient models available.

Electricity

Unless you are fortunate enough to have the means and the know-how to generate your own electricity, you will have to pay for someone else to generate it. In some parts of the country, electricity tends to be very expensive. Regardless of where you live however, that monthly electric bill can be substantial. But the good news is that we are billed for what we use, so there is probably some room for savings if we reduce our usage.

Probably the easiest and least painful way to cut electricity costs is to simply turn things off when not in use. When you leave a room, switch off the light. Encourage family members to shut off the TV when no one is watching. And the same applies to computers and electronics. When cooking and baking, plan your activities so that you piggy-back your oven usage. Reheating a cold oven takes a lot of power. Know what you want to get out of the fridge before you open it, and get everything out at once. Each time you open that door, the fridge has to work to replace the cold air that escaped. I call all of these activities as "passively limiting usage" because you're not giving up anything, just eliminating wasteful habits.

The next step I refer to as "aggressively limiting usage." This requires some adjustment (not sacrifice) as to what we do. For example, reduce the wattage in light bulbs. Can you get by with a 60 or 75 watt bulb rather than 100 watts? A further savings is to replace incandescent light bulbs with compact fluorescent ones. A word of caution here: Compact fluorescent lights are much more expensive than the old fashioned incandescent. Consider replacing them only as the incandescents burn out; to replace them all at once would be an unnecessary cash outlay and you may not recoup your savings in the short term.

Is it possible to lower the temperature of your hot water heater? For those in colder climates, consider insulating your hot water tank, and even putting it on a timer rather than having it heat water when no one uses it.

Appliances that have their own dedicated circuit are power hogs. That's why they have their own circuit. If you can reduce usage of these appliances you will see significant savings. The first one is your range. Plan your meals so that you use the microwave instead of the regular oven. Another is your clothes dryer. On nice days, is it possible to hang your laundry outside? I know that this not an option for everyone because many condo and homeowner associations prohibit clotheslines in backyards and on balconies. But manufacturers still make folding drying racks. Use those as much as you can.

For those who want to save, look into cost saving measures from your local power company. Many have programs where by agreeing not to use major appliances during peak times, you will be offered a monthly discount. Others have voluntary programs where you try to stay within budgeted kilowatt usage. Make sure you completely understand how these programs work because if you exceed usage, you may be hit with a surcharge. These programs are not for everybody.

Whatever you do, don't go out to buy new energy saving appliances if there is nothing wrong with the existing ones. You'll end up using your precious cash that you may need for other things down the road. Once you regain your footing; i.e., get another job, then you can make the investment. Frankly, I would replace them only when needed, even if I had a good job. Only if I could prove significant savings or recoup my investment rather quickly would I consider doing it.

Electricity Usage on the Tiers:

Moderate

Turning off appliances, electronic equipment, and lights when not in use is common sense, but we don't always do it. Make an effort to click it when you leave it.

Motivated

Replace lights with lower wattage bulbs, or replace them as they burn out with compact fluorescent lights. Plan your meals so that you use the microwave oven rather than the conventional oven. Wrap your hot water tank, and put it on a timer. If possible, dry your clothes on a line instead of a dryer.

Extreme

Contact your power company to see if it has any cost saving programs where you voluntarily agree to limit usage. Make certain you understand the program and its implications before you sign up.

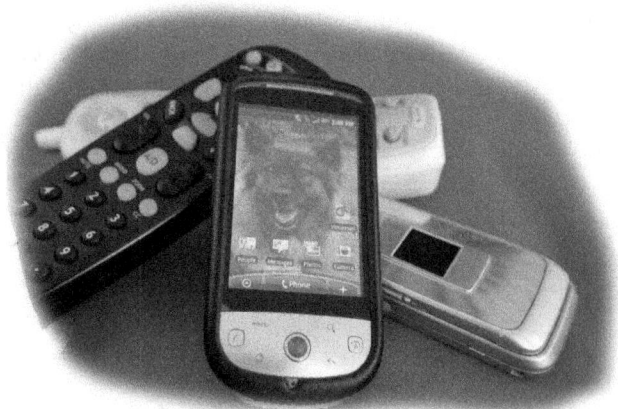

Communications

Gone are the days when we used to have just a telephone bill. For many, gone are the days of even having a telephone. Nowadays phone companies bundle local phone, long distance, internet, cable TV, and mobile phones into one whopping bill. Talk is not cheap.

Phone: There are a myriad of plans out there, and I can't even begin to cover them all. However, if you still have a land line, look at your plan. If you are charged for long distance calls based on usage, then obviously make fewer calls and make them shorter.

Call your phone company and ask if there are alternatives. For example, when we signed up for phone service, we selected an option that best suited our needs at that time, which included unlimited long distance calling. Since then, our long distance calling has dropped tremendously, and when we do make long distance calls, we tend to use our cell phones. Why pay for it when we don't use it? We dropped that feature and saved ourselves a nice chunk of change on a monthly basis. Speaking of long distance, there are some internet-based long distance companies that offer incredibly cheap rates. Check into those.

Lastly, ask yourself if you even need that land line. There are people who have never had a land line; they grew up with a cell phone in their hand. If you think you can get by with just a cell phone, drop the land line. You may have to modify your cell phone plan to compensate, but you may still be way ahead by having only one phone bill rather than two.

Internet: The plans for this utility generally are not as flexible and do not provide as many options as phone plans. And in your area, you may be limited to only one internet provider. However, it may be worth your time to call them or check out their website to see if they do offer a plan that might save you money. When a communication company is in business to make money, why should their representatives call to offer you a cheaper plan? But if you ask and if they value your business, you may be able to take advantage of plans offered to new customers. Also look on the internet to see if there is an alternative to your current provider. Be forewarned though: Changing a provider may cause you to change your email addresses, and that could be very time consuming.

Cable TV: I would consider this a luxury, but in that thinking, I may be in a small minority. Most people consider satellite and cable TV a necessity. Therefore, I'm including it in this section.

Cable companies typically charge a flat rate based on level of service rather than usage. If you're looking to save, take a look at the plan you selected. See what's included and consider how many of those channels you watch. Compare your plan with the others the provider offers. Can you get by with a lesser plan? Only you can make that decision, but if you need to save you may be willing to make the sacrifice.

If you really want to save money, drop the cable or satellite TV completely. What, no TV at all you ask? Not necessarily. Local broadcasters send signals over the air. You would need to get an antenna which you can buy at Radio Shack or other comparable retailer or even over the internet. If you have an older TV set, you'll need to get a digital converter as well. And there you go, you've got free TV; the way it used to be when I was a kid!

Also, most of the major networks make many of their shows available for viewing over the internet. And other websites offer other shows, such as Hulu.com.

Mobile Phones: Cell phones, mobile phone, iPhones, smartphones – whatever you call them, you have to pay to use them. Some offer prepaid plans; others you pay by the minute or by the kilobyte; and still others by level of service provided you stay within parameters. The easiest thing to do is to examine your plan and look at your bill. If your plan includes 500 minutes per month, and you're using 600, then you're paying through the nose because those extra 100 minutes are at a premium rate. If you don't want to change anything, then stay within your plan. Monitor your minutes, the number of text messages, and data downloads (usually measured in kilobytes or megabytes).

Carriers such as Sprint, Verizon, and AT&T offer different levels of plans. If you find yourself exceeding your plan limits, then call your provider to see if you can change your level of service. Paying for the higher level might be cheaper than paying for service overage.

Although it's generally less of an issue nowadays, by all means avoid roaming charges. If you are out of your provider's coverage area, turn off your phone until you are back within the network. This is the safest way to avoid roaming charges. You don't want to pay dollars per minute to have your buddy ask you what's up.

Most carriers have contracts for their service, typically one or two years. Once your contract is up, check out the competitors to see if they have lower rates or better plans. You may even ask your current provider for any promotional offers. There is no incentive for your current provider to call you with better offers when they can just bill you at your regular rate. Make the calls and check out the websites. If you have to, create a chart to make it easier to compare prices and features.

Use your current phone until it breaks or you have a new job. As tempting as it may be to have the latest and greatest in your hand, this just isn't the time to buy a new cell phone, even if there is a rebate (with a contract, of course).

The biggest saving would be to terminate your cell phone plan, provided that you're not under contract. You don't want to pay that termination fee. You may want to opt for a prepayment plan and use it very sparingly, such as for emergencies. Or you may want to just get rid of it entirely, like some people I know. They decided that having a mobile phone was unneeded and unnecessary. Think how much money every month that would save you! This is an extreme measure, and for most people this would not be an alternative, especially if you don't have a land line. But if you are one of those independent and strong minded individuals, then I applaud you. Make sure, however, that you have a land line with an answering service or a phone with an answering feature. You don't want to miss any calls from potential employers.

Bundles: Most communication companies will provide savings if you go with a bundle. This makes it difficult to compare if you are looking to change providers or if you want to drop some services. And it becomes even more complicated because not all companies carry all services. Some companies, like AT&T, offer all services from phone to cable to cell phones. Others offer fewer services, such as Sprint that offers only cell phone and air card services for internet. Create a chart and list all services and the cost for each. This will make it easier to compare, particularly if you are changing from one company that covers all services to another that offers fewer services. You'll need another provider if you want to replace the missing services. Additionally, make sure you ask about ALL fees. You'll have to pay taxes, connectivity charges, FCC mandated charges, and a plethora of other made-up fees that do nothing but gouge your wallet. Get all the fees before you switch. You want to avoid the hassle of changing providers only to realize a miniscule saving after the taxes and additional fees.

Communication on the Tiers:

Moderate

If you are paying for long distance minutes, then make fewer calls and keep them short. Note what channels you watch to see if you can switch to a lesser plan without sacrificing your favorite TV shows. Make sure you stay within the limits of your cell phone plan, and avoid roaming charges.

Motivated

Carefully examine your phone plan and remove features seldom or never used. Check for better deals for your internet provider. Drop your cable or satellite TV service to its lowest level. Shop around for a cheaper cell phone plan.

Extreme

Either drop your land line completely, or give up the cell phone. Terminate your cable or satellite TV plan and use an antenna to pick up free over the air signals. Watch some of your favorite shows on the internet.

ENTERTAINMENT

We all can agree that entertainment is not absolutely essential to live, but it would be hard to completely give up. It is only human to want to have fun whether it's playing a computer game, playing the piano, or playing sports. To many people the idea of fun means interacting with others, so we also do things such as socializing with friends, becoming members of organizations, and even participating in competitions.

The benefits of entertainment are limitless because they engage us, expand our minds, allow us to relax, and permit us to see and experience new people and places. Doing fun things makes life worth living. Unfortunately, many of these activities also cost money, and that's a problem when we're unemployed. Nobody is telling you to sit in the corner and count the cracks in the ceiling; that would be like a prison sentence. You still need to interact with other people, relax, and have some fun. The challenge is to do it while conserving your money. It's not impossible, and you may discover new ways to just have fun.

The definition of entertainment is as varied as those who enjoy it. One person's idea of entertainment may be considered dreadfully dull by another. Someone else's idea of a good time may be climbing Mt Everest. In other words, there are too many forms of entertainment for this book to list. But if you look at the major categories below you may get ideas of how to save money whatever your idea of having fun.

Dining out

Most of us will agree that the past few years represents the toughest economic period we've experienced. But you wouldn't know it when you enter some restaurants to find out there is a 45 to 60 minute wait for a table. It's just the way our society has evolved; good times with friends and family center on food. And it would take a truly serious economic catastrophe for the pattern to stop. On a smaller scale, realize that you're going through an economic catastrophe of your own, and you may need to change your dining-out habits.

The check for a family of four at a moderately priced restaurant can easily come to $200 or more when you include appetizers, desserts, taxes, and tip. If wine and drinks are ordered, then add another 30 to 35% to that bill. That's a lot of money to spend for two hours. How long did it take to earn that much money? Also think of it this way: That's almost half of your unemployment check! Going out to eat is a huge drain on your precious capital.

The easiest way to save on dining out is to simply find less expensive restaurants. You don't have to compromise on the quality of food, but perhaps you can select restaurants that have a homier feel than the latest trendy ones. If being out with friends and family is the important thing, then the ambiance of the restaurant may be less important. Neighborhood restaurants also offer excellent foods at a fraction of the cost, plus you may get better service

Some restaurants offer two-for-one deals where you get two entrees for the price of one. Usually restrictions apply, so ask your server to make sure what you ordered is part of the special. Also look for coupons. Restaurants will sometimes offer coupons in mailings or even on websites featuring specific locations, cities, downtown areas, etc. Many restaurants offer early-bird specials. Yes, these are popular with retirees, but if you want to go out to dinner, early-bird specials are substantial savings, and some include soup, salad, and dessert. Plus the early bird hours at some restaurants might actually be late enough to almost coincide with your normal dining time. So you eat a bit earlier; small sacrifice for big savings. Check websites, flyers, and ads for other deals ahead of time.

I generally skip the appetizers, and just about always do without desserts when I go out to eat. If you have a small appetite, order an appetizer as your meal. Better yet, order a regular portion and only eat half and take the other half home for another meal the next day.

Desserts in particular can make a moderately priced meal become much more. And have your coffee at home! Paying $3 for a cup is insane when you can make it in your kitchen for pennies. Also a huge cost cutting measure is to have your alcohol at home and just stick to plain old tap water when you get to the restaurant. For the price you pay for a single cocktail or a glass of wine, you can buy a whole bottle for home. And speaking of water, avoid the imported bottles of water and just ask for tap water with ice.

You know your finances the best, but if you've only got funds to last you only two or three months, then you shouldn't be going out to eat much at all. If you do decide to go out as a break from the routine, settle for a diner or fast food. Don't forget the coupons though.

The biggest savings, of course, is simply not dining out. Or if you go out once per week, make it once per month instead. Remember, food in a restaurant is going to cost more than buying your own food. Even fast food restaurants aren't that cheap any more. A fast food meal for four, assuming a combo meal for each, can easily come to $32.00. For that amount, you can make a very nice dinner for four, or better yet, make burgers and pocket the savings. And from the earlier example of a moderately price dinner for four totaling $200 without drinks, that would buy groceries for a week.

With all of these cost-saving measures outlined here, there is an exception. If you think going out to dinner may lead to a job, then by all means go. For example, if you know your friend's company is hiring, going out to dinner with him or her could be a way to get your foot in the door. And if your friend is willing to "put in a good word for you" consider picking up the tab in appreciation, as long as the bill is reasonable!

Socializing

It's human nature to get together with other people. Just because you are unemployed doesn't mean you have to become a hermit. Frankly, you should be doing the opposite and socializing more. Use this as an opportunity to network. But use caution; you don't want to go broke while partying.

Dance clubs and popular night spots are not cheap. If you're getting together with friends in these places, then keep a few things in mind:

- Get there early to avoid paying the entrance fee (if there is one). Yes, it's uncool to arrive that early, so go hide in a corner and text other friends while you wait.
- Make your drinks last by sipping them slowly. Or buy bottled water or sodas; they're cheaper.
- Don't buy rounds! If you're with true friends, they will know your employment status and shouldn't expect you to buy their drinks.
- Go out less frequently.

You could socialize at home by inviting your friends. Use caution though – don't turn this into a party. Hosting a party means you buy the drinks, snacks, mixers, etc. That will end up costing you more than if you had gone out. Make it an informal event with friends to play cards or video games, and where people can bring their own drinks. The is nothing wrong with saying it's BYOB.

Look to substitute more expensive social outings with cheaper ones. Pot luck dinners, church suppers, picnic outings can all be fun and relatively inexpensive. If you have the space in your home, you could even host such an event.

Dining Out and Socializing on the Tiers:

Moderate

Look for less expensive restaurants where you can still enjoy a good meal. Get referrals for good neighborhood restaurants. Skip appetizers, desserts, and coffee. Reduce what you spend for "nights out" by drinking less, not buying drinks for others, and avoiding entrance fees.

Motivated

Dine out less frequently. Look for coupons and other deals such as two-for-one and early-bird specials. Have your drinks at home rather than at the restaurant. Plan social events at home such as game nights or informal BYOB get-togethers.

Extreme

Avoid dining out, or consider eating at diners or fast food restaurants. Try going out to less expensive social events such as pot luck dinners or church related events.

Ticketed Events

I'm grouping any event that requires the purchase of a ticket, such as games, plays, shows, or concerts into this category. Tickets for some of these events may be available only by subscription as well. Whether it's a ball game or the ballet, these events are generally pricy, and should be considered unnecessary while you are unemployed – particularly if you are buying tickets for a whole family. Of course, if you purchased tickets or a subscription before losing your job, then by all means attend, or if you're being frugal minded, maybe you can sell your tickets.

I know there are die-hard sports fans and supporters of the arts out there. You know who you are, and you'll probably end up buying those tickets regardless of what your conscious is telling you. So, for those folks, the savings would be what you do when you're there. Rather I should say what you DON'T do. Once there, don't spend another dime. Eat before you go so you'll not be tempted to buy hotdogs. Forgo the drinks at intermission. Find parking at more distant garages, or if possible, take public transportation. In other words, it shouldn't cost you more than the price of the ticket(s) and getting yourself there.

You might want to consider cheaper tickets. Make the sacrifice of not being behind home plate or front row orchestra. Do your homework: Most venues have websites that show seating sections and corresponding prices. Even if tickets are only available at the box office, print the layout before you go to help you make an informed seating decision. There are websites out there that offer deep discounts for sporting and cultural events; however, they are usually for the day of the event. Examples include Tickes.CheapTickets.com, www.LastMinutePass.com, and Tickets.us.LastMinute.com. Be wise and compare prices between the venue itself and the discount website before making any purchase.

Many ticketed events are by subscription or by the season. So why not buy a subscription with a friend and split the cost as well as the tickets. This will only work with good friends, but if you can work out who sees what and when, then this is a good compromise. It's not like airline tickets which are issued for a specific person.

If you're truly being frugal and there's an event or a series you want to see, look into volunteering for the organization or venue. You could be an usher or serve in some capacity for the organization, such as stuffing envelopes or whatever. Usually volunteers can attend performances for free. This may not work for all cultural and sporting events, but it's worth looking into.

There is always the option of not going. In this case, it's the easiest option, but it's also the biggest sacrifice. If it's a sporting event, maybe you can watch the game on TV, and some cultural events are recorded and available for viewing later, or even simulcast on radio. The bottom line is this: Do you spend $100 per ticket, or do you buy groceries? It's up to you, but I'd rather skip a concert than skip a utility payment. And remember, your situation is temporary; you'll be able to get to that game or concert soon enough.

Ticketed Events on the Tiers:

Moderate

If you must see that concert or that game, then go, but don't spend another dime. Don't buy any foods or drinks while you're there. Skip the t-shirts, programs, and other drains on your wallet. Find cheaper parking at more remote lots.

Motivated

Research the seating plans and buy cheaper tickets. Consider splitting a subscription with a friend, another couple, or another family. Look for last minute tickets online.

Extreme

Bite the bullet and forgo the event; watch it on TV or if possible, view a recording later. Volunteer for the organization or venue in order to see or attend for free.

Movies

Movies...the most popular and common way to experience a story. The only three older ways are from plays, books, and storytelling. Spinning a good yarn and enjoying that story make us human. We've been doing it ever since we became civilized; it's ingrained in us. We love stories, particularly when they are acted out and filmed in Cinemascope and Surround Sound. Like everything else, we have to pay for them.

I needn't remind you what a movie ticket costs. Our parents and grandparents can tell us stories of when they would spend all Saturday afternoon at the movies for a dime. Today making a movie costs between $10 to $100 million, with some as high as $175 million. Air-conditioned theatre complexes with comfortable seats, sophisticated sound systems and the latest projection technology guarantee that 10-cent movie admissions are a thing of the distant past. According to the National Association of Theatre Owners, the average ticket price in 2010 was $7.89. Ticket prices in my area are $10, but for a national average it's safe to assume by now it's $8, which means to catch a movie with a family of four (two adults and two teenagers) now costs $32. Popcorn and sodas will run the total to over $50.00. Hope your comment on the way out wasn't "the book was much better," otherwise you might as well just have taken that $50 bill and thrown it out your car window.

Like everything else discussed in this book so far, how do you save money and still maintain your standing in the movie-going human race?

For starters, skip the popcorn, candy, and drinks. Those prices are crazy, and what's even crazier are the people who buy them. You can't tell me you can't be without junk food for two hours. Eat before you go. If you have to drink something during the movie sneak in a bottle of water. Look at this way: Going to the movies with a family of four costs $32.00, and at least another $18.00 for sodas and popcorn. Skipping the sugar water and the palm oil will save you 36%.

Be more selective about the movies you see. Why pay top dollar to see a film of marginal interest. Or, if you go weekly, cut back to once every two or three weeks. Again using that family of four analogy, $32.00 per week times 52 weeks is a whopping $1,664. Half of that is $832, and a quarter is $416. The good thing about numbers is that they don't lie. Going to the movies 13 times per year as opposed to 52 times results in a 75% savings.

Another easy option is to hit the matinees or early morning times. Depending on the theatre, savings can be as much as 50% depending on the time and day of the week. Other days and times the saving is only 25%. So if you must see a movie, go in the mornings for the 50% savings. You can still talk as intelligently about the movie as those who paid full price.

The biggest savings occur by not going to the theatres. I have to remind you that your employment status is temporary, and it's not as though you can never go back to the movies later on. It's just right now when you've got little or no income.

You can avoid theatre prices by renting movies. You can be in the comfort of your own home, make your own popcorn, and adjust the sound to your own liking. You can even make a social event out of it by inviting a few friends to watch with you.

There are still some brick and mortar buildings that rent videos and many supermarkets have machines that dispense movie disks. The cost is less than the price of a single matinee ticket.

If you're a big movie buff, then join NetFlix or BlockBuster. Staying on the lower levels of these memberships will roughly be the monthly cost equivalent of two adult tickets. If you want to sign up for the higher membership levels, that's fine, just do it AFTER you've landed that new job.

Movies on the Tiers:

Moderate

You don't have to miss that movie you've been waiting to see, but you can do without the popcorn and sodas.

Motivated

Cut back your movie going. Matinees are a good deal; motivated people will hit the theatres during the mornings to save as much as 50% of the ticket price.

Extreme

Avoid the theatres entirely while you're in your job transition and rent your movies instead. For those who enjoy many movies, then join the lower levels of NetFlix or BlockBuster.

Vacations and Travel

My initial inclination in writing this book was to not put vacations on the tiers. The reason is quite simple: You should not be going on vacations while you're unemployed. Period. Vacations are a luxury and a reward after a prolonged period of hard work. Yes, I know you are working hard to find that next job, and I know that being unemployed and searching for a job can result in a high stress level. But a vacation right now means thousands of dollars, and a family vacation doesn't make any economic sense. A week-long vacation may end up costing as much as three or four months' worth of living expenses. You may be confident that you'll find a job, and you probably will, but you just don't know when. It could be more than a year away. You may need that three or four months' worth of money to live, but if you've blown it on a vacation, then what do you do?

I can hear those "buts" coming in. "But I've got to go see my mother in Texas." "But the kids have to see their grandparents over the holidays." "But we always go to our yearly family reunion." You get the idea and you you've probably got your own "but." I understand that there are family obligations; there are weddings. Sadly, people do get ill, and worse yet, die; and parents do age and require life changes. These are reasons why you may need to travel in spite of your financial condition. What should be avoided are trips solely for pleasure. Reward yourself when you've accrued enough vacation time with your new job.

You might also consider traveling solo. If the reason of the trip is not a major event, is it possible for the unemployed family member to make the trip while the rest of the family stays at home? It's far cheaper for one person to make a trip than four. Whoever you're visiting is someone obviously close, so I'm sure they'll understand why you made the trip by yourself.

Lastly, before you go ahead and book a trip to your cousin's wedding, seriously and honestly ask yourself if you truly have to go. Some of us are close with our relatives and living far away does tend to make the heart grow fonder. So are you using your cousin's wedding as an excuse to see the rest of your relatives? Do you have other siblings who live closer than you do to help out with an aging parent's short-term illness? Is it vital to attend your nephew's high school graduation? If you think about it and you feel doubt about the wisdom of going, or if you feel guilty about spending your money, then your answer is not to go. Don't make the decision by yourself – ask your spouse, parent, or whomever you're close with. After deliberating, if you are sure the trip is worth the expense and you are convinced that it's the right thing to do, then go. You should avoid making unnecessary trips just because "it would be nice to be there."

So if you must travel, consider the costs. The biggest is lodging followed by meals. Don't forget the airline tickets, and car rental. But it doesn't stop there; you've got to include the price of admission to whatever attractions you want to visit, and then there are incidentals such as gasoline, tolls, taxis, souvenirs, and other drains on your wallet. Incidentally, this analysis is for U.S. and Canadian travel only. Although many concepts may apply to international travel, there are other concerns such as safety, language barriers and local customs, health issues regarding food, and other potential problems which are all beyond the scope of this book. My best advice for traveling to lesser developed areas is to use common sense; don't risk your safety or health just to save money.

Lodging: Let's consider each category starting with lodging. Depending upon where you go, lodging can run in the hundreds of dollars per night. Certainly New York City is among the most expensive with $400 per night being a bargain.

If you're driving, plan your trip and book your room(s) in advance. Try to pick places near bigger towns and where there are several hotels in the immediate area. It's possible to find out by searching hotels and the name of the town. You'll get an idea if you see multiple hotels with similar addresses, or better yet, located on a web-based map. By booking in advance, you eliminate the possibility of rooms being nearly sold out with just expensive ones left. Even if you are flying you can do the same for hotels near your destination.

You can also look online at websites listing last minute hotel deals. www.Priceline.com, www.Hotels.com, and www.Expedia.com are examples. I found www.Kayak.com to spider across the above websites and more, so you'll get a much larger selection of options. The prices these websites list may or may not be discounted. The only way to tell is to call the hotel and ask what their rates and compare.

Should your destination be in a larger city, you might want to look for lodging in the outskirts. Downtown hotels charge premiums, and you may have to pay for parking in addition. Just make sure you are in a safe area; you may have to do research.

The best deal is to stay with friends or relatives. I can't speak for your relationship with your friends, nor can I comment on your personal needs, but if it can work out, then try it. Remember, you are in someone else's home, so be careful, cautious, and considerate.

Meals: Please refer back to the section on dining out, but keep in mind that when you travel you have fewer options. Eating in probably won't work unless you are staying with family or close friends. If you are staying at a hotel, check to see if there is a supermarket close by. Most hotel rooms have a small refrigerator and a microwave oven, so it is possible to eat at least one meal in your room. For the other meals, go for fast food places and be selective as to what you order (i.e. salads over greasy burgers and fries), or go for regular restaurants and look for specials, coupons, and early bird deals.

Airline Tickets: With one exception, which I will explain later in this section, avoid booking at the last minute because you'll pay top dollar. Book as soon as you know that you'll be traveling. And try to be flexible with your dates. Flying on the weekends will cost you more than flying mid-week. Use the internet to make your own airline bookings. Be flexible with your dates and times, and try several combinations. Try changing the date of departure by a day either way (i.e. one day sooner and one day later), and do the same with the return. If it means a 40% savings for airfare for a trip that is one day less, it's a no-brainer. Don't try to justify staying that extra day.

Use websites such as Travelocity to start your flight search. Remember that not all airlines are affiliated with those sites, and some only offer tickets on their own website. So, find a good fare on the travel site, and then check the websites of the few airlines that don't participate. You'll know which ones are missing; there are fewer than a dozen domestic major airlines.

The only exception to last-minute travel is to look at websites offering drastically reduced airfare for the last minute. If you're completely flexible and probably going to fly single or with just one other person, this is doable, maybe not so much with a family or for people with physical disabilities because you may end up with red-eye flights, long layovers, or other unpleasant traveling woes. Check websites such as www.CheapOAir.com, www.LastMinuteTravel.com, and www.FareBuzz.com amongst others for last minute deals. I would also check the individual airline websites to compare prices.

Car Rentals: Once you've made your airline reservations, start looking at car rental rates. Use websites that list daily or weekly rates for several rental companies, which makes it easier to find the best deals Usually, smaller cars are the best deals, so go for those. You may hate subcompacts, but you're not buying it, you'll only be using it for a short time. Deal with it and pocket the savings. Check with your auto insurance agent to make sure you're covered when you rent a car. Usually that extra insurance is unnecessary and expensive. Also, take the option to fill the gas tank yourself. You'll find gas sells for much less at stations than what the rental agency will charge.

Other costs: Unless you're familiar with the destination area and know short cuts and secondary roads to avoid tolls, stick to major highways. You can't negotiate the tolls, but to venture off interstate highways to avoid the tolls may lead you into slower stop-and-go traffic and frazzled nerves.

If the point of the trip is to spend time with friends and family, then you should not be sightseeing. We all know touristy areas are a drain on your wallet; stay away from them. If you do venture out for some sightseeing – and it would be hard not to do so if you've got children with you – be selective. Leave the souvenirs in the gift shops.

Traveling on the Tiers:

Moderate

Plan and book your trip in advance. Look for the best deals for your airfare and car rental. Look for lodging where there is a lot of competition and away from city centers (or airports) so you can get a better rate. Buy food at a local supermarket and have at least one meal in your room.

Motivated

Be flexible with dates when you book; fly mid-week and stay over a weekend if you can. Rent the smallest and cheapest car. Try to stay with friends or family. Avoid dining out as much as possible even if it means offering to buy groceries. Stick to the purpose of the trip and don't go sightseeing.

Extreme

If the trip is not an emergency or one with a planned event, such as a wedding, look into websites offering last minute deals. See if the trip can be made by one person rather than the whole family. Ask yourself if the trip is absolutely necessary.

Hobbies

This is an old term: hobbies. Nobody uses that word anymore, but there's no single word to replace it. "I'm really into painting" or "I love mountain biking" or "I do photography" are phrases that essentially mean hobbies. Whatever you want to call your passions, creative outlets, or pastimes, these should not be exempt from your money-saving mindset.

Some crafts and hobbies are very expensive, but for different reasons. Digital photography can be expensive because you need the camera, lenses, flashes, etc. Once you have most of this equipment, going out on a photo shoot, unless you're hiring a model, should be minimal. So for such hobbies, provided you already made the initial investment, you can continue to use this equipment at minimal expense. However, this is not a good time to make such initial investments.

On the other hand, traditional photography can be expensive on an ongoing basis even after the initial investment for equipment. In this medium, you have to buy the film, processing chemicals, and photographic paper. These products were always expensive, and now that most people use the digital format, there are fewer suppliers, which means higher prices. For this hobby, I would recommend seriously cutting back.

If you've got an "expensive" hobby and you decide to scale back, does that mean you have to sit there and twiddle your thumbs in the evening? Of course not. I'm sure you have other interests, and this may be a good time to explore them. Remember though, look for hobbies, crafts, and activities that are inexpensive. One of the cheapest activities is reading. Libraries still exist, but for those who are connected with the digital age, you can download free books from Amazon.com, where there is even an e-book lending program.

As for outdoor activities, there is no reason to stop. Hiking, biking, swimming, etc. are all terrific things to do, and they're good for you. But rather than driving two hours to go on a trail, can you find one that's only 20 minutes away? Or can you carpool with several others to cut the gasoline expense? As for swimming, assuming you don't have free access to water (i.e. a public beach) and you typically pay to use a pool, are there lower-priced options during the day as opposed to the evenings? Put the same principles to use with other activities I may not have mentioned, like tennis.

Other outdoor activities are just plain costly. Golf comes to mind, as does skiing. Greens fees and lift tickets can be incredibly expensive. For these expensive activities, look for cheaper alternatives, such as public golf courses or secondary ski areas. Or significantly cut back on the frequency you golf or ski. Better yet, scale back and only go to less expensive courses and ski areas. It's not forever.

One note on golf: A lot of business is conducted on the golf courses. If you think that there is a good chance of networking and meeting people who are in a position to hire, then you may want to continue this activity. Don't limit your chances of finding a job just to save a few bucks. Save money by cutting back on something else.

Hobbies on the Tiers:

Moderate

If you already made the initial investment in a craft or hobby, (i.e. already bought the equipment), and there is little expense in enjoying that activity, then go ahead and continue enjoying it while you're out of work. Don't make an initial investment in a new hobby. If you enjoy outdoor activities, find ways to minimize the expense, such as carpooling or looking for off-peak times.

Motivated

If you enjoy several hobbies, stick to the less expensive ones during your period of unemployment. Should your hobbies be expensive ones, then scale back by engaging in them less frequently. For golfing, skiing, and other expensive outdoor activities, look for alternative venues such as public courses or off-peak times.

Extreme

Switch to less expensive creative outlets, or give up the expensive hobbies during your period of unemployment. Look for ways or angles where you could perhaps turn your favorite activity into an income producing one. See Part IV for more thoughts on this.

EDUCATION

Tuition for private schools and colleges is no laughing matter, even when you're employed. Chances are that you or your family made some hard choices when deciding on the program of study, how to pay the tuition, and even selection of the most appropriate school or college. Now that your income has been eliminated or drastically cut, paying for education becomes even more daunting. The money you use to pay tuition could seriously cut into funds that you'll need for things like mortgage, insurance, and even food for the months to come. Unless you've already have funds set aside for tuition, you may want to look at some alternatives.

529 Prepayment Plans: Tuition prepayment plans are a smart idea for the long term, but they offer limited benefits in the near future; this means it generally makes more sense to enroll in a 529 plan when your child or beneficiary is very young, rather than waiting until he or she is in high school. The plan also allows others, such as grandparents, to make contributions. Obviously the bulk of the funds come from parents.

If you find yourself unemployed during the earlier years of such a plan, you have more flexibility because your unemployment is temporary and in the long run should have little effect. During your unemployment period, you can contribute the normal amount, a reduced amount, or nothing. Only you can decide, based on your needs, which option would be the best fit. However, it might be wisest to contribute at a reduced rate.

Later in the plan, such as when the beneficiary is in high school, you may not have as much flexibility, particularly if you joined the plan later in the beneficiary's life. Your decision will definitely have an impact on your future tuition payments and/or the choice of college. Depending upon your cash situation, it might also be a wise idea to continue making payments at a reduced rate. Making no payments or contributions at this point will have much more of a long-term effect. But, check the details of your plan to make sure there are no penalties for changing or skipping monthly payments.

Private Schools: If your child or children are enrolled in private schools, you have an added large expense over parents who send their children to public schools. You may have made the decision to send your children to private schools based on religion, quality of education, or proximity to home; however, now you are faced with a large expense and reduced income. Many private schools are locally owned and managed, so perhaps a visit to the financial officer could result in a temporary negotiated tuition reduction, or the administrators could point you to programs and resources to lower your tuition costs. You will have more clout if you have more than one child enrolled in the same school. Otherwise, you always have the option of public schools or home schooling.

College Tuition: Quarterly tuition payments can be painful. Unlike private schools, most colleges and universities offer little or no flexibility in tuition, so you pay or your child (or whoever is going to college) can't attend classes. It's not to say there aren't any other options.

Being unemployed is not shameful – it happens to millions. Call or visit the financial aid office and tell them that you lost your job. Because your income level has dropped, you or your student may qualify for assistance in grants and or scholarships that had been previously denied. Once enrolled, colleges and universities prefer keeping their students rather than having them drop out due to financial problems. Because of your economic situation, administrators may open up reserved or emergency scholarships. Keep in mind that you may have to show proof of your financial situation, such as a letter from your previous employer stating that your job was eliminated. There are no guarantees that the college or university will provide any assistance, but the likelihood does exist, and therefore it's worth asking.

Should the college decline to offer any financial assistance, or if you suspect that your period of unemployment will be long, or you get the indication that your next position will be at a much lower salary, then you may want to consider sending your student to a less expensive school. Private colleges and universities are far more expensive than their state counterparts. Switching schools at mid-education might be an alternative if:

- You can find a similar program of study at a state college
- The state college will accept the former school's credits
- The student won't lose any financial assistance, grants, or scholarships
- There will still be a significant savings after incurring costs associated with changing colleges, such as moving expenses, deposits, and other charges.

If you're faced with the unpleasant choice of tuition payments or mortgage payments, there are still some options. Student loans would shift

133

the burden of college tuition, at least part of it, from you to your student. You can always help your student make the loan payments later on.

You may be able to make an IRA withdrawal to cover education costs without paying an early withdrawal penalty. Of course, if this is a traditional IRA, then you will incur a tax liability, however, it this is an option to help cover educational expenses. If you decide to try this option, I strongly urge you to talk with a tax accountant or financial professional before you make any such move.

There is also the possibility of borrowing the funds from family members or close friends to cover tuition while you're out of work. This is a touchy area, and many people do not feel comfortable asking friends and relatives to borrow money; conversely, many don't like being asked. Only you can judge whether this is a viable option. If you do borrow money, make sure it's in writing and you stipulate the loan amount, when and how it's to be repaid, and if there is any interest. This will help keep any potential problems at bay.

If you're paying for a dependent's tuition plus living expenses, it may be time for the student to get a part-time job while in school to help defray these costs. Making a summer job a must will also help, provided that the wages are saved.

Graduate schools are more negotiable than under graduate schools. Again, a call to the financial aid office to discuss your financial situation is a must. Depending on the program of study, graduate schools offer fellowships where the student will proctor exams, grade assignments, and even be an assistant teacher in return for the aid.

Finally, if there is no other choice, the student may have to temporarily suspend the education. If you decide on this option, make sure you speak with the school's financial office to see if there are any ramifications.

Other Education Expenses: This includes private lessons such as music lessons, tutoring, and extracurricular activities. You are the best judge in this matter. If it's something that your child absolutely needs to be successful in school, then continue with it. For example, piano lessons for a child prodigy who probably will have a career as a pianist makes sense. Inversely, paying for piano lessons for a child who is merely interested in learning as hobby should be temporarily suspended. It's your call because it's your cash.

Education on the Tiers:

Moderate

Talk to administrators of private schools for tuition reduction, or see if there are any resources to assist with tuition. Encourage your college student to apply for more grants and scholarships now that your income level is reduced. Call the financial aid office and discuss your employment situation; you or your student may qualify for additional financial aid. Find out if your graduate student qualifies for any fellowships. Temporarily reduce payments into 529 plans.

Motivated

If needed, temporarily enroll your children in public schools while you're unemployed. Defray college expenses by making your student assume more responsibility for his or her education by working part time or during breaks. Temporarily suspend payments into 529 plans if it's permissible.

Extreme

Look into transferring your student from a private college to a state college or university. Have your student take out student loans or borrow funds to cover tuition while you are unemployed. Consider the possibility of withdrawing funds from an IRA to cover tuition and other educational expenses. If If those options are not viable, then look into temporarily withdrawing the student from college

PETS

Being unemployed does not mean we have to give up our pets any more than we would have to give up our children. Okay, okay, I heard some of you ask, "You wanna bet?" Whether you keep your kids is up to you, but I hope you do. And as far as pets, I hope you keep those as well.

Dogs, cats, birds, and other pets provide us with unconditional love, joy, and companionship. They are also a responsibility, and of course, like everything else, pets cost money. They need to be fed, they get sick, and they need shots, which mean trips to the vet, which sometimes can be very costly. And they need to be groomed. But like most other expenses, there are ways to save.

Pet food: Unless your pet is on a special diet, you may want to consider changing to a cheaper brand of food. Should you decide to do this, gradually transition from the old food to the new. Abrupt changes in diet could cause your pet to have stomach or digestive problems. Also compare ingredients with the current brand and the alternative brand. You know your pet better than anybody else, so if you think the cheaper brand will keep your pooch or kitty in good health, then try it. Just remember, they can't tell you they've got a tummy ache.

Veterinary Services: If you're like me, once I find a professional service provider that I truly like and trust, I tend to stay with that provider for a long time. That is the case with my current vet, and I'd prefer not to change to someone else because if there is a problem I can count on him. Unfortunately, he's not cheap, and I know that there are other vets in the area who offer their services at a reduced rate. So, what do you do? Well, it's up to you. If it's a matter of necessity to spare every dollar, then go with the cheaper vet. It's pretty clear. Just make sure you have references, meaning that you know people who take their beloved pets to that new vet. Ask these people if they are happy with this vet and if they've experienced any negative issues. And remember, you can always go back to your preferred vet when you get a new job.

I am reluctant to take our older dog to a new vet because he's got some health issues and I want the consistency of a regular vet who knows the dog's history. Should there be a problem, he'll have all necessary background information, and I have a good rapport with him. So, when there is a medical issue, I ask him what it will cost. I also eat crow and say, "You know, I'm unemployed and have been for quite some time. Is there a cheaper alternative?" Sometimes there is a cheaper alternative, and sometimes he takes some charges off the bill. I don't expect that every time I go, but it's worth asking. In all honesty, I'd rather not say that and just pay the bill and grumble about it on the way home, but when we're unemployed we've got to put the pride aside.

There is another matter worth discussing in regard to your pet and veterinary services. At some point there will probably be a serious health condition with your beloved pet. Hopefully, this won't happen while you're out of a job, but should it happen, it's best that you be prepared. Heaven forbid you are told that your pet needs an expensive procedure. What do you do? Well, again that's up to you. We've all heard stories that someone's pet needed surgery to survive and the bill ended up at $5,000. Then the pet died three months later. I recommend is that you get as much information as you can: prognosis, likelihood of reoccurrence, the effect of your pet's age, and the ordeal your pet will have to endure. Also do the math: Get an estimate of the TOTAL cost (including x-rays, tests, blood work, etc), and compare that to your available funds. Remember, your funds need to cover you and your family for your period of unemployment. If you haven't already, this would be a good time to mention your employment status to see if your vet can offer his or her opinion. It's a tough shot to call, so don't make a snap decision. It's very difficult, but try to remove emotion from the decision process. Ultimately, I'm sure you'll do the right thing.

Grooming: Cat owners are lucky – their pets are usually self-cleaning. Dogs, however, are not. I always bathe ours in the back yard with the hose. He hates it, but he would probably hate it much worse having a stranger do it. And I would hate paying for it. I know that many pet owners don't want to be bothered bathing their dogs; in all honesty, it's not much fun and I usually end up taking a bath as well. So I can see their point.

You know there is a "but" coming, and here it is: But you need to cut expenses, and if you have the capability, then give your own pet a bath. If you have a small dog, the shower, bathtub, or even the sink will work. Larger dogs usually need some outdoor space. It's unlikely that you can bathe your

St. Bernard in your tub or shower without your whole bathroom becoming a flood zone. If you can, however, do it yourself and pocket a $20 to $30 savings.

Trimming is even more costly: from $40 to $100 or up depending on the size of your pooch. Ask yourself if it's absolutely necessary. Our dog is long haired. He was born that way; my thought is that he doesn't need to be short-haired, so I don't have him trimmed. I brush him regularly to remove the tangles and keep him looking good.

Or can you do it yourself if you want your dog's fur trimmed? Hair clippers are relatively inexpensive and come in kits with a variety of different length guards. In all honesty, if you goof a little bit, your dog is hardly apt to complain, unlike trying to cut your teenager's hair. The savings are considerable.

If you decide you can't bathe or trim your "baby" then try to find a cheaper groomer. There are many out there, including bathing services at pet motels and chain pet markets such as Petco or Pet Supermarket.

Pets on the Tiers:

Moderate

Find cheaper alternatives for your pet's food and grooming. If you need veterinary services, ask for cheaper alternatives, and don't be too proud to mention that you're unemployed and on a tight budget.

Motivated

Find a veterinary center that charges less. You may have to look further away than your current vet. Make sure you get referrals before you try this new place, or at least try it out with minor services.

Extreme

Bathe your own dog. Suspend trimming your dog while you're out of work, or try trimming him yourself. Make major decisions regarding your pet only after you have considered all medical and financial aspects, and remove emotion from the process.

YARD AND GARDEN

Most of us agree that the appearance and upkeep of the exterior of homes is a reflection of the folks who live there. Just because one of the breadwinners lost a job does not mean that the yard and garden has to go to seed. It's important to keep your home looking good.

Remember though the key word is "maintaining" and not "redoing" or "redesigning." To maintain should cost no more, and ideally less, than what you were paying while you were working. This is not the time to spend money to redo the yard or garden. Also, many people enjoy gardening as a hobby or passion, and there is no reason to change that. The only difference is now it's on a financial shoestring.

Lawn care: During warm months, lawns need mowing. It's a fact of life. Northern climates require fewer months of the chore and of course, in the extreme south, the job has to be done year-round. Nonetheless, this requires either effort or money.

If you have a lawn service, your physical effort is none, but it costs you. In my neck of the woods, a cut costs between $25 to $35 every two weeks. Over a six-month period, that totals to $325 to $455. If you are physically capable of doing it yourself, then you've got a little jackpot of savings; except you might have to buy a lawnmower. If you decide to do it yourself, don't buy a new mower; get a used one. Check your newspaper or Craigslist.com; or talk to your neighbors. Chances are that someone gave up on mowing themselves and there's an older, but working mower that's not being used. When you regain your income, go back to your lawn service and sell the mower; if you're lucky you'll be able to sell for what you paid.

If you're not up for the task of mowing – and it is hard work as I know firsthand – then you can always look for other lawn service companies that'll give you a better price.

Shoveling and Plowing: This is one of the main reasons we moved to Florida! Yuck! Having lived most of my life in New England, I do know what shoveling is. It's hard labor; probably worse than mowing. Again, if you're physically fit, do your own shoveling. And as with a mower, look to buy a used snow blower if you have a large driveway.

Should shoveling be too much for you, try to negotiate a better rate for plowing and shoveling. When we are working, we are sometimes too busy to shop around, especially if we've been using the same company or person for years. You now have time to look for a better deal. And if you do, maybe the "guy" you have now may be willing to meet a competitor's price. Who knows; it's worth asking.

Hedge and Tree Trimming: Unless you've already been doing these tasks on your own, I wouldn't advise starting now just because you're trying to save money. Unless you have smaller hedges or small trees, these activities require specialized equipment, training, and ladders. In other words, the safety risks increase tremendously. A fall from a ladder or a severed finger does not justify the savings. Your best bet in saving money here would be to shop around for the best prices and to stretch the time between trimmings; i.e., instead of six trimmings per year, try four. Chances are that no one will really notice.

Pleasure Gardening: I'm including into this category such activities as planting flowers, pruning, mulching, etc. This is a common passion that many find relaxing and rewarding, myself included. There is no reason to give up your pleasure, but you might want to consider ways to save money, at least while you're out of work.

Plants are not cheap, especially perennials. Instead of buying new plants, why not take cuttings, split the roots, or other forms of propagation? Swapping cuttings with friends is an excellent way to cut back on plants that have overgrown and gets you some new ones. Growing your own plants from seed is rewarding and can be used to as a learning experience with kids.

A packet of seeds costs about $1.29 and provides potentially dozens to hundreds of plants. And finally, if you do buy plants, buy them small; a plant that is 6 inches tall and sells for 99 cents will grow to be the same size as the one that is 3 feet tall and sells for $14.99.

A bag of mulch is not a major expense, but 50 bags can easily become a $100 purchase. If you know you're going to need a lot of mulch in the near future, look for sales at Lowe's or Home Depot. You might also call lawn and garden centers because you can sometimes buy mulch in bulk for considerably less. Sometimes cities or towns offer free mulch as a way of getting rid of cut vegetation, so keep your eyes open. Finally, old leaves and grass clippings also work as mulch, and that's usually free. It may not look as pretty as store bought, but you can't beat the price!

Yard and Garden on the Tiers:

Moderate

Shop around for the best quotes for mowing and plowing services. Look for gardening sales at Lowe's or Home Depot.

Motivated

If you are physically capable, do your own mowing and shoveling, but check with your doctor if you're unsure. It's hard work, but think of it as your workout for the day. Plant from seed and use cuttings and other forms of propagation to increase your plant stock.

Extreme

Take the Motivated tier to the Extreme by using those measures plus getting free mulch or making your own. An added benefit is that it's also a "green" thing to do.

HOLIDAYS AND GIFT-GIVING

Holiday Gifts

There never is a good time to be laid off, but there are times of the year when it is worse than others. A tough time to be out of work is during the holidays. I know of families who started to decorate their homes and stopped abruptly when the breadwinner was laid off shortly before Christmas. It can be devastating, and it can ruin the holidays.

Having gone through bouts of unemployment during the holidays myself, I can speak from experience. The good news is that your employment status doesn't have to ruin the holiday season; it just means it's going to be different.

Holiday gift-giving for some people is nothing more than an obligatory drain on the pocketbook, while others enjoy shopping for hours to find the perfect gift for each recipient on the list. Regardless of your approach, it's important to understand where gift-giving falls in your priorities. Obviously food and housing are basic needs, and, therefore, are more important uses of your limited cash. So is paying your health, life, and auto insurance. You need to maintain your car, and have gasoline to get to your interviews. You'll also need to keep your home heated, pay your utilities, and make your payments on your car and credit cards. Okay, so we all agree that gift-giving falls fairly low in the list of priorities.

I can't speak for all of you. I'm sure that there are some who have the fortitude and foresight to say no to holiday gifts. Others will cut back and only give a few token gifts to immediate family, while others will scale back only minimally. For the latter, this may be due to family dynamics and a question of pride when gift-giving, especially to extended family members is out of duty or obligation rather than genuine devotion. Even if you want desperately to give gifts, it's important that you at least limit them because they negatively affect your cash.

That being stated, I know some of you are going to give gifts regardless. That's okay, but for your own sake, please temper your generosity. Here are a few ideas to help you save face and your bank account.

- Look for bargains, sales, and discount stores. Can you get it online at a cheaper price (but don't forget to consider shipping charges)?
- Instead of giving two or three gifts to each person, give only one. Remember the old cliché: It's the thought that counts.
- Cut out the extras. By extras, I'm referring to things like stocking-stuffers, gifts attached to other gifts such as a box of chocolates in addition to the main gift, joke or gag gifts, or impulse and last-minute gifts.
- Examine your list of recipients to see if you can equitably cut some. For example, can you tell your extended family something like, "You all know that I'm not working at the moment and I need to save money. So this year we are only going to give presents to the children." This may not work in every extended family situation, but no one will fault you for thinking of the nieces and nephews before your own siblings.

Speaking of children, holidays are a special and exciting time for them, and especially for your own. I doubt any parent would willingly forgo presents for their kids. Gift-buying on a shoestring is easiest for toddlers because they would be happy with most anything. They have no concept of where the toy came from, whether it was a deep discount store, online, or even used – within reason. You probably don't want to buy used toys if the child is apt to put it in his or her mouth. Older teens, at least in theory, have a better grasp of understanding issues, and if you are honest with them, they may be somewhat gracious with the token gift you bought them. Children in between toddler and older teenage years are more difficult because they are more apt to feel slighted that their holiday haul was less than their friends. They are also more knowledgeable about brands, and the latest trends and fads, and would want to keep up with their friends. There are no easy answers here; either you shell out the money or they are unhappy. All I can suggest is cutting back to one item.

Another gift suggestion is to give what is needed. It may not be what your child would want, but if it's needed anyhow, why not wrap it and put it under the tree.

If you are creative or good with your hands, can you make your own gifts? Personally, I tend to appreciate a gift even more when I know someone's put their heart and soul into it. But make sure you know what you are doing before you begin such an undertaking. Starting a new craft from scratch can be costly. And even if the recipient likes home-made items, I can probably say with certainty that no one likes a sweater with one sleeve longer than the other, unless they have the arms to match.

There are gifts that cost you nothing and would probably make the recipient very happy. How about if you give a promise of a service? For example, you can baby sit for a couple with a young child, or invite someone for a nice dinner, clean your parents' house or garage, do the laundry for a month, or even help with a laborious task. Be cautious, however. Make sure you know what you're setting yourself up for. Also, make the extent of your gift clear by presenting the recipient with a nicely printed "certificate" of what you intend to do for that person, and when, and how much, etc. Plus, the certificate can be wrapped and opened like any other present.

And speaking of wrapping, why not cut back on the paper itself? Over the last few years, wrapping presents has become an art form. There's nothing wrong with that when one is working, but when one isn't, the old-fashioned way is more economical. Look for the large rolls of wrapping paper at discount stores and don't' worry that all of your gifts are wrapped in the same paper. Skip the ribbons and use inexpensive bows. The markup on wrapping paper, gift bags, ribbons and bows, and all other related items is incredible. Why part with your precious dollars only to help make huge profits for some nameless corporation? Half of your recipients won't even notice because they're more interested with what's inside. And even if they do notice, it's only going to get ripped off the box and thrown away.

Giving token gifts is another way to cut the holiday expense. If you're close enough to give them presents, you are close enough for them to understand your situation.

Finally, you can always bow out of gift-giving. You are the best judge of your finances, and if you think that buying presents will jeopardize your well-being, then by all means skip the gifts. True friends and close family members will certainly understand. Unfortunately, you may have to brace yourself against talk behind your back by selfish and inconsiderate people. Chances are those same people would talk about you regardless whether or not you gave them a holiday gift.

On a side note, if you decorate for the holidays, use what you already have. Don't buy new decorations. If they were used the previous year, and you didn't throw them away, they are probably good enough for this year.

Holiday Gifts on the Tiers:

Moderate

Look for bargains and sales for your gift buying. Buy only one gift per person and cut out the extra gifts such as stocking stuffers. Put a dollar limit on all gifts.

Motivated

Cut back on the number of recipients. Give only needed items to your immediate family, and for others, give token gifts. Limit how much you spend on wrapping paper, bows, etc.

Extreme

If you're talented or creative, make your own gifts. A nice gift would be a service that you can perform, such as babysitting. Consider sending cards with your good wishes rather than giving any gifts at all.

Other Gifts

There are many other events throughout the year where giving gifts is expected. These include birthdays, graduations, religious events (bar/bat mitzvahs, first communion, and confirmation), weddings, quinces, and anniversaries. Some of these occasions are a once-in-a-lifetime event and are meant to be memorable and special. Religious events signify major milestones in becoming an adult within the congregation. Others occur yearly, such as anniversaries and birthdays. Many of these occasions are acknowledged with some sort of gathering, and of course, gifts. Religion, family traditions, and even local customs may dictate the type and amount of gift.

Being a part of a large and extended family or having a wide network of friends can result in many invitations to such events. For these people, gift-giving can become a significant expense even for those who are gainfully employed. But without income, these events can seriously drain your capital.

So what do you do?

If your extended family and your social network are smaller, then the number of these events will also be less. Assuming you have enough cash in the bank to cover yourself and your family for six months, then gift-giving is not so much of an issue, and you can continue to give gifts as you normally do.

However, if you are down to only a few months' worth of reserves, or if you are frequently invited to events, then it may be time to reconsider your gift-giving.

There are no easy answers or solutions, but when it comes down to feeding your family or buying gifts, the choice is fairly clear. Here are some suggestions.

Limit all gifts to a set amount, such as $25 or $50. If you are fair-minded, then you will feel less guilty giving your nephew Bobby's $25 for his birthday when you also gave $25 for Bobby's older brother for his bar mitzvah.

Another way is to draw circles around your immediate family, another one for very close family and friends, and then maybe another circle for family and friends you like. So, for those who are outside any circle, even though you may like them, you send a card; those in the outermost circle, a small gift. Those in the second circle, a better gift, and you reserve your largest gift for those in the innermost circle. Whatever you do, don't reveal your gift-giving strategy because that may cause friction.

You can also cut the number of events to which you will give. For example, you can decide to hold off on birthdays, but continue to give wedding gifts or for other once-per-lifetime events.

Depending on your relationship with the person who is celebrating a milestone, you could always give him or her an IOU. This does not mean you'll put an IOU note in the card, but you can say that you'll make it up to them once you regain your income. This may not always work, but if it does, don't forget your promise later on.

Lastly, comes the option of not giving. You should acknowledge the event with a card inscribed with a few words. Whether you mention your financial condition is entirely up to you. Remember, if you are close enough to want to give a gift, then the recipient or the recipient's parents should already know about your employment status, and they should understand.

There is another form of gifts that should be discussed: donations to charity and contributions to religious organizations.

Charitable donations are extremely important in our society because many organizations do wonderful work with the disadvantaged. Many do not get any government aid and rely solely upon donations to exist and carry out their work. Without donations, many of the recipients would face insurmountable problems.

Charitable donations can take on many forms. Some will send you reminders, calendars, candles, and even coins and postage stamps to get you to mail them a check. Others come door-to-door. Some of you may mail a check out of the blue or on a regular basis to your favorite organizations. Donations can also take the form of clothing, furniture, and even old cars. Even giving loose change to street musicians constitutes donations.

If your reserves will last you six or more months, you can continue to make your charitable donations as you always did. However, do not start new ones. We all get solicitations in the mail with heart-wrenching photos of disadvantaged children, people who are starving, and dogs and cats who need medical treatments. Even when you are working, you can't give to them all. Now that you're not, you certainly can't add more charitable organizations to your list.

Should your reserves be for less than six months, you should consider cutting back on your donations. This can be done by donating only to your favorite organizations, or you can donate to all of them, but cut the amount.

If your reserves are very low, then this is not the time for any donations. If you do have clothing or old furniture to give, then you can give them in place of cash. But, make sure you don't give items you'll need because this is not the time to replace things.

You can always suspend all donations during your unemployment period. Trust me; you'll get plenty of reminders in the mail once you resume working.

The same applies as religious contributions. Parishes, synagogues, and congregations cannot survive without member support. Without sticking my nose into your faith, you need to consider your financial situation before blindly contributing.

If you think you've got enough reserves to last you throughout your unemployment period, then go ahead and make your normal contribution. Remember, though, there is no way of knowing how long it will take before you get your next job.

Reducing your contribution is probably the most logical thing to do. You can still be active in services and in the congregation, and you should not feel guilty. Your life drastically changed when you were handed your pink slip, so this is just another facet of that change.

Should your resources be near the end, you may want to consider other ways to support your congregation. You may want to discuss this matter with your priest, rabbi, or pastor; it may be possible for you to volunteer your time and effort rather than your cash. This will still keep you connected with your religious community and not feel like a freeloader. If anything, you'll have much more contact in your community which could lead to a job opportunity, and a better sense of spirituality.

Some congregations are very literal on tithing, and that can put you in a negative situation. Strictly speaking, you would have to contribute one-tenth of your unemployment benefits. That can be quite a bit on a monthly basis; enough to buy a week's worth of groceries. I would recommend a conversation with your pastor. If there is no resolution, it may be time to find another congregation – at least on a temporary basis. I can't make this decision for you, but remember that charity begins at home. When it becomes a matter of survival, you come first.

Gifts and Donations on the Tiers:

Moderate

If you have few invitations and reasons for gifts, then continue to give as you normally do. Otherwise, set a limit on the amount of gifts.

If your reserves are adequate, continue making charitable and religious donations as you normally do. Limited reserves, on the other hand, may mean cutting your donations to charities and religious congregations.

Motivated

Only give gifts to close friends and family, or be much more selective as to which events you will give.

Make charitable donations to fewer organizations or cut the donation to all of them.

Extreme

For appropriate occasions and with some people, you can always make it up to them later by deferring the gift. You always have the option of sending a card with your best wishes. There is no law that says you must give a gift.

Temporarily suspend your charitable donations while you're unemployed. This is a temporary situation, and you'll have plenty of opportunities to give in the future.

Talk to your minister, rabbi, imam, or priest to see if you can volunteer in your organization in place of your cash. If you find yourself low on money and the congregation is inflexible to your situation, you may need to find another one for a while.

PART II – BUDGETING

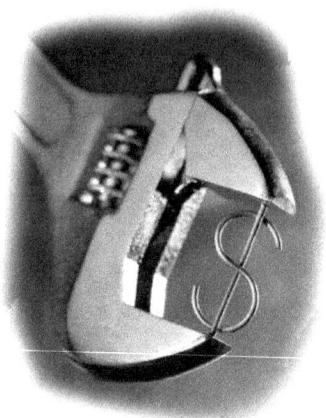

Often the best tools in life are the simplest: a hammer, a wheel, a knife, and a budget. Yup, a budget ranks right up there with the discovery of fire, electricity, and even the computer. It truly is a powerful tool, and one that most people love to ignore.

Granted, the term "budget" doesn't bring pleasurable connotations. Maybe you were laid off because of "budget cuts." We've all heard the politics about "balanced budgets." We've seen examples of corporate budgets that ramble on for pages on end. But really, a personal or family budget can easily fit on a single sheet of paper or a computer spreadsheet. It doesn't have to be fancy or full of $20 words. But, the service it provides is immeasurable for two basic reasons: First it helps you save money, and second, it helps you stay out of debt. It's priceless, and it's easy. You can do it!

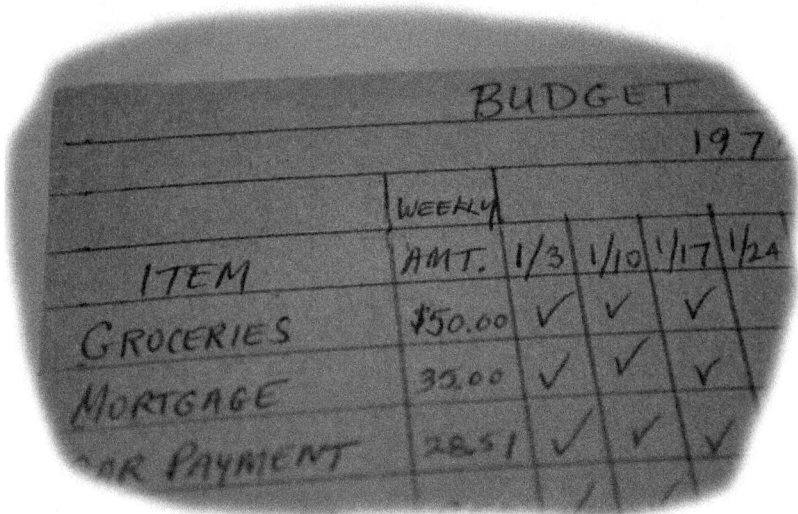

A Story

When I was a kid, which to me wasn't that long ago, my Mom controlled the family finances. She wasn't an accountant; she didn't even go to college, but she was certainly smart and savvy about money. She had to be; we were a family of four living on my dad's very modest salary. One tool she used to make money stretch was a budget.

Every Friday Dad would stop at the local credit union (not a bank – they are for-profit organizations and charge unnecessary fees) to cash his paycheck. He would request lots of small bills and coins, and he would hand this over to Mom. After dinner she would pull out a strong box that was full of labeled envelopes and a manually drawn grid on a piece of cardboard. This cardboard grid was the checklist; in effect the budget. All expenses were listed along with the weekly amount that she would put into the appropriate envelopes. She knew how much to spend on groceries each week. Electricity costs were calculated by taking a monthly average and dividing by 4 to get the weekly amount. Car insurance, which was paid annually, was divided by 12, and then by 4 to get the weekly amount. In effect, all expenses were broken down into a weekly amount, and all expenses had a corresponding envelope. That way, when the bills arrived in the mail, there was sufficient money to pay them. As she placed the weekly amount in the corresponding envelopes, she checked the column on the grid.

I know you have two questions after reading this last paragraph. I'll answer the first one now. Why did she do that? Why didn't she have a checking account instead of using cash? Back then, checking accounts were not free, but using cash was. Fortunately, we never had a fire and our home was never burglarized. She kept a lot of cash on hand, and that proved extremely helpful in case of emergencies. Banks and credit unions kept normal business hours back then and typically were closed on weekends, and there were no ATM machines, let alone debit cards.

The other question that may have been bugging you is that you may have noticed that all expenses were broken down on a weekly basis with four weeks to every month. If you do the math, then you'll see that comes to 48 weeks in a year (12 months times four weeks per month). What happened to the other four weeks in the year? Not to worry, she knew what she was doing. Those months that had five weeks were treated just as any other week. That created a surplus in all of the envelopes. Why? Well, even back then prices were increasing, so for some expenses the "extra" weeks were to offset inflation. Other envelopes, such as for fixed expenses such as car loans, the surplus was used to either pay down the principal, or as a form of additional money for savings. She monitored all expenses and amounts set aside. Depending on the envelope, the surplus was kept there, taken out and put into a small slush fund for unexpected expenses, or put in their savings account.

All through my growing years, never once did any of us go without any essential item. We always had good food, decent clothes, gasoline in the car, etc. We did not, however, have skiing trips, piano lessons, or other luxuries; there was a limit to how far my Mom could stretch those dollars.

Incidentally, while Mom was "doing the budget," Dad was looking at supermarket circulars planning meals based on sale items, clipping coupons, and preparing his all-inclusive shopping list which he would use on the following morning. After they both finished, they would sit back and enjoy a much deserved cocktail while my kid sister and I watched The Brady Bunch.

Real Life

No one is expecting you to budget the way my mother did. Even Mom changed her ways; later on, when I was in college, the local credit union offered free draft accounts (their version of checking accounts), and she dispensed with the strong box. However, she kept a modified version of the cardboard checklist. This helped her determine how much she needed to keep in the checking account at any given moment to cover the bills. Some of the aggregate surplus was divided between contributions to their IRAs and a regular savings account, and the remainder stayed in the checking account for contingencies.

That cardboard checklist was actually her budget. That was one of her best money management tools. That and her ability to find bargains, knowing the value of money, and overall ingrained Yankee frugality enabled them to survive tough economic cycles of the mid-to-late-70s, and meet their maker with a sizable nest egg left over.

I am living testimony that budgets work. Frankly, they are essential to good economic stability. Most companies, and certainly all publically held corporations, prepare budgets. The reason is very simple: Investors want to know where the company is spending their money. It also makes it clear as to where they can cut expenses and by how much. So why not employ the same tool to make you more economically sound?

Okay, I hear you; what good is a budget right now while I'm unemployed? Yes, a budget is normally used when you have a regular income, but frankly using a budget can show you where you can save money, and a good budget can even tell you how long your nest egg will last while you're out of work. Plus, it's a good habit to get into once you start working again because it will help keep you out of debt.

Budget Basics

Simply stated, a budget lists all your income and all your expenses. The key word is ALL. And for both categories.

Income consists of your salary (net salary), your spouse's net salary, income from part-time jobs, unemployment compensation, Social Security benefits, alimony, child support, veteran's benefits, pensions, interest paid to you, and any other payments including welfare. Your bother-in-law's repayment of a loan is not income, that's capital replacement.

Expenses include anything you pay out. This includes food, rent or mortgage payment, clothing, electricity, heating oil or natural gas, car insurance, gasoline, car payment, credit card payments, dining out, movie tickets, and even your daily stop at the coffee shop. Expenses are harder to list because there are a lot more of them, and most people don't track all of them, particularly those "tiny" purchases, although they should.

The concept is very easy: Total your income, and then total your expenses. Ideally, the income should be greater than expenses. I used the word "ideally" because for most people, expenses exceed income, even when everybody in the family is working. That's typically because most people are bridging the gap with credit cards, which only incurs more and more debt. But that's a topic for another book. For now, the focus is on making your nest egg last, so let's get started on your budget.

Step One: List your income. As already stated, this is your net salary or unemployment compensation, your spouse's income, and any other family member's salary who is contributing to the income pool. Also include benefits such as pensions, Social Security, alimony, and child support if those are applicable. Don't forget to include rental income if you are a landlord. Should you be fortunate to have interest income, be sure to include that as well.

Step Two: List your expenses. This step will require you to do more work, because let's face it, there can be a lot of them. But remember, the more accurate your budget it, the more meaningful it becomes, so give it your best shot to list ALL your expenses. To help you make your list, think about what you normally do on weekdays. What's your routine? When do you reach for your purse or wallet? Then think about what you do on weekends, and add those activities to the list. You might also want to look back through receipts, bank statements, credit card statements, checkbook registers, debit/credit card slips, etc. You might also want to go back in time if you keep records. Some expenses show up only quarterly or yearly, as opposed to daily, weekly, or monthly.

Step Three: What do you do with all of this info? The first thing is to organize the data so that it means something. In this step, separate the items you pay on a regular basis from those that you paid just once. For example, your electricity bill is something you pay every month, but that receipt for a handbag or a box of golf balls is a one-time expense. Smaller piles are easier to tackle than larger ones, so make two piles, one for regular payments and one for the "once-in-a-while" payments.

Step Four: This is an easy step. Create a blank spreadsheet or get a new sheet of lined paper; in either case, this is your "grid." From the pile of recurring expenses, determine which ones are the same every month. Enter them and their monthly amount into your grid. These include rent/mortgage payment, car payments, alimony/child care payments, etc. Don't forget those things that you pay annually or semi-annually, such as real estate taxes, homeowner's insurance (if those aren't paid from an escrow account), or vehicle taxes (excise tax), etc. Divide yearly bills by 12, and semi-annual bills by six. Quarterly bills should be divided by three. Enter the monthly amount on their corresponding lines. If you have a bill that you pay every week, and it's the same amount every time, then multiply it by 52 and divide by 12 (this gives you a more accurate monthly amount rather than multiplying the weekly amount by four because some months have five weeks).

When you have finished listing these expenses with their amounts, leave a couple of blank lines or rows in case you think of more. This first group of expenses is called your fixed expenses because the amount you pay each time (weekly, monthly, quarterly, yearly) is always the same. Below are some typical fixed expenses:

- Rent/mortgage
- Quarterly homeowner or condo fees
- Car payment
- Credit card payments
- Alimony and/or child support
- Car insurance
- Health insurance
- Homeowner's/renter's Insurance (if not escrowed)
- Real estate taxes (if not escrowed)
- Vehicle registration and taxes (usually yearly, so divide this by 12)
- Cable/satellite TV
- Medications
- Regular medical/dental office visits

Step Five: Pull from the pile the bills or expenses that change every time, which are called variable expenses. For example, your electricity bill is not the same every month, and your grocery bill is unlikely to be exactly the same from week to week. Add these expenses to the list, but leave the amounts blank for the moment.

Don't just use the last amount paid for a variable expense. Because the amounts are different each time you pay them, the logical thing to do is to enter an average. Let's take groceries for example. If you shop once per week, then it's easier. Take the last six weeks' worth, total them, and then divide by six. For example, if your grocery bills were: $147.03, $161.99, $155.10, $139.29, $157.16, and $165.88, then the total of all six is $926.45. Now divide that total by six for an average of $154.40833. I like to round up to the nearest dollar, so in this case, the weekly average is $155. To get the monthly average, multiply by 52 and divide by 12.

If you shop as you need things, or you shop almost daily, then this might be more work. Try to pick a "typical" month when you tended to stick to your routine and you had no unusually high or low grocery expenses. For that month, make sure you have accounted for all supermarket trips from either the receipts or from your bank statements. Total those receipts and then ask yourself if this total is truly representative of what you spend each month. If it sounds about right, use it. If you think you've probably not accounted for all trips, then make your best guess and enter that number for your monthly food expense.

Should you be a record freak like I am and you shop as needed, then add up three months' worth of these receipts and divide by three. This will give you a very good average grocery bill.

Do the same with other expenses that change. Keep in mind that some expenses will run higher or lower depending on the season. Let's take electricity for example. If you heat and cool your home with electric power, then you bills might be higher in January than in May, and might be again higher in July than October. Taking the average of six months' worth of bills will give you an accurate figure to use in your budget.

Also, consider your expenses right now. If you drove 50 miles each way for your job and you're now laid off, then it doesn't make sense to include the higher gasoline expense in your budget. Look at what you've been spending for gasoline since your termination and get an average from that.

To help you, here is a list of variable expenses:

- Electricity
- Telephone/cell phone
- Groceries
- Heating fuel
- Municipal utilities (water, sewer, trash collection, etc.)
- Gasoline
- Household goods
- Health and beauty aids
- Unusual medical/dental expenses

Step Six: From this pile, find the items that occurred only once, such as the bill for the electrician when you had a shorted outlet replaced, the receipt from the doctor's office for a special visit, and the receipt for the new tires. Organize these into home repair and maintenance, vehicle repair and maintenance, healthcare expenses, etc. These expenses occur only when needed. Either go back in time to get a monthly average for these expenses, or do your best to estimate a monthly amount. Enter those expenses and amounts into the grid as well, and then leave a couple of blank lines for the next grouping of expenses.

Step Seven: Now look at the rest of the pile, which should now be much smaller. These should be expenses that vary from month to month, or for goods and services that didn't fit in with the variable expenses. You might be wondering why I didn't include things like beauty salons, sporting events, dinners, gifts, etc. with variable expenses because many of these do vary. Well yes, they do vary, but these are considered discretionary expenses because they are not needed to live. Granted phones aren't needed either, but you have to draw a line somewhere between living a normal life and buying luxury items.

There may be some flexibility as to how you classify a few expenses. For example, clothing wasn't listed as a variable expense, although no one will argue that you need clothes. Realistically, most people probably have enough clothes to carry them through a period of unemployment. Therefore I put clothing in the discretionary group. But if you have dependents who are growing and need clothing for school, then this becomes a variable expense. The idea is to create a realistic budget to help you see down the road. You won't get a knock on the door from the budget police if you split your clothing expenses between two groups. After all, you know your own expenses better than anyone else. The point I'm trying to make is that there is a difference between a pair of shoes for your child and a pair of designer shoes for yourself; your child needs those shoes, but you can probably live without the Pradas.

Other expenses, such as dry cleaners, hair salons, or church contributions can be classified as variable or discretionary depending on several circumstances. For example, dry cleaning would easily be classified as variable if you want to keep your business suits looking sharp and fresh for interviews. It becomes discretionary when you decide to send several items to the cleaners just because you've not worn them for a while. The same applies to salons if you opt for a service beyond what you normally get.

Either use the actual monthly amount, an average, or an estimate of each expense and enter them in your grid.

Here is a list of discretionary expenses as a guide. It's by no means complete; only you can do that:

- Dining out
- Trips for coffee; sodas and snacks at the convenience store; beers at your favorite pub
- Hair salons and barber shops
- Movies and movie rental subscriptions
- Sporting and cultural events
- Gifts
- Magazine subscriptions
- Gambling (including lottery tickets, betting pools, and bingo)
- Hobbies

Okay, the worst is over; take a break and then go on to the next step.

Step Eight: Total your income.   Then subtotal the three groups of expenses and come up with a final total. Compare your total income with your total expenses. Ah, now you've got some hard facts staring at you.

In an ideal world, you would be working, and your expenses would be less than your income. Unfortunately, we live in a less than ideal world, and I'm willing to bet your expenses exceed your income. Probably considerably. But, that's to be expected because you or your spouse is out of work, and even if you are collecting unemployment benefits, most likely it's only a fraction of your old salary.

So you think to yourself, "Well big deal. I knew that already; I didn't need to go through this exercise to figure that out!" Of course, that's true. But now let's put the tool to work.

First you now know exactly (or at least fairly close) what it costs for you (the "you" here includes yourself, your spouse, your dependents, and your household) to live every month. When you subtract your total expenses from your income, you get a negative number, or to make it sound a little better, a shortfall.

To keep things going as they are, somehow or other, you've got to cover that shortfall. If you had been a squirrel and stored some nuts in the bank, then of course you would be using that cache of cash to make up the difference. So, let's take this one step further. To see how long your stash will last you, divide your bank account balance by the monthly shortfall. For example, let's say that Joe and Maria prepared their budget just as you did. Joe was laid off from his job and is collecting $1000 per month of unemployment benefits. Maria works part time and brings in $750 per month. Assuming no other revenue, their total monthly income is $1,750. Their total expenses come to $3,000 per month. Their shortfall every month is currently $1,250. They have $6,000 in the bank, so that money will last 4.8 months ($6,000 divided by $1,250.) They can survive for just under five months before their money runs out.

When you are dealing with facts and figures, you are forced to face reality. The "I think I'll be okay" now turns into "I will be okay" or "Oops, I'm not at all okay." The doubt is gone. This is one main reason for preparing a budget.

Going back to the Joe and Maria example, they know they have to withdraw $1,250 every month. They both think that it may take much longer than 4.8 months for Joe to find another comparable job. If they want their $6,000 to last longer than 4.8 months, they have to reduce that monthly shortfall. They have a very powerful tool right in front of them to help find ways to cut expenses; it's listed right in their budget.

The first place to look for cuts is that discretionary expense category. Those are the expenses that aren't necessary to live, remember? When Joe was working, he was making a good salary, so they enjoyed several dinners out each month. Although they thought they cut back after Joe got his pink slip, they discovered that they were still spending $250 to dine out each month. Maria was spending $125 per month on bingo outings and lottery tickets (and like the rest of us, not really winning). Joe is into professional sports and was spending an average of $250 per month for tickets and for beer and food at the games. Maria was taking private Tai-chi lessons twice per week at $30 a pop, for a monthly average of $260. They also were shocked to find out that they were spending an average of $75 for movies and associated food and beverages at their local cinemas. Cutting these discretionary expenses saved them $760 per month, which now means their monthly shortfall is $490. Now their $6,000 nest egg will last more than 12 months ($6,000 divided by $490). And in today's market, being unemployed over a year is not uncommon.

Joe and Maria feel somewhat better knowing that their savings will cover them for a year. But they decided to be cautious and not deplete their savings even after a year. Things do happen; washing machines break, car parts need to be replaced, and people get sick. So, they decide they need to cut more corners to really preserve those dollars in the bank. The next round of cuts would be in the variable expense category. Because they are committed to living as close as possible to a balanced budget (i.e. expenses less than income), they will find ways to cut in groceries, utilities, gasoline, etc. They may even try the Tier approach!

Joe and Maria are of course fictional people. You are a real person living in a real world. You may not have been able to sock away $6,000. You may not have had the money to go to professional sporting events, have private Tai-chi lessons, or spend $250 per month to dine out. But you do have a real budget in front of you, and you've got the information in Part I in your hands. Take a look at your discretionary and variable expenses to see where you can save. The lower your shortfall, the less you have to withdraw from savings or worse yet, borrow. Forcing yourself to account for all of your money will clearly show you where you can cut. Go back and review Part I and see if you can't apply some of the techniques to lower even your fixed expenses. Try moving up to the next tier on more expenses to wring out more savings.

Budgets also have tremendous value when you're back at work. Many working people don't realize that they are spending more than they make. They don't realize that they are filling that gap or shortfall with credit card debt, and that's a nasty trap. So once you get that next job, continue with your budget to help keep you out of the debt trap.

Also, do yourself a huge favor by adding an extra fixed expense. You need to pay yourself! I omitted that expense in the discussion above because when you're unemployed, it wasn't relevant. But once you're back in the workforce, you need to pay yourself for your efforts. That should be 10% of your income, and it should go into the bank. Why? You can never tell what life may hand you, and having money in the bank can smooth out the rough spots.

PART III – MORE SAVINGS AND PITFALLS

Here is a list of topics that can help you save additional money. They don't fit well on the Tiers, so I put them all together in this part. If there are topics that don't pertain to you, then feel free to skip them. I won't be offended. However, for the sake of being more enlightened, why not read them all?

Bulk and Membership Club Stores

I'm a big advocate of stores like Costco, BJ's, and Sam's Club. I've had a Costco membership for over 14 years, and when a BJ's opened near home a few years ago, I bought that membership as well. These stores offer great prices, and coupled with their coupons, the savings are even greater.

But these places can be dangerous when you're out of work. Heck, they are dangerous even when we are working. The reason is quite simple: We can easily get carried away in these stores. They offer better quality products and good food at a fraction of the cost elsewhere. And we all know that many of the items they sell, particularly the display areas in the center of the stores, are one-shot deals. Once they sell what they've got, the likelihood of seeing a particular item again is slim. So we snatch these items up thinking we got a great deal. And perhaps we did, but those things weren't what we were going to buy in the first place. It's very easy to end up buying way more than we originally intend. And when we're unemployed, that's not good.

There are other concerns with these warehouse stores. First, they charge a yearly membership fee; usually a basic membership is about $50 per year, or $4.17 per month. To come out ahead, your average monthly savings by shopping there has to be greater than $4.17. Remember, you should be buying only what you need, not the things you want, so make sure the savings on those few things you buy are greater than the membership costs. For my household of two, I can justify both memberships rather easily.

If you already have a membership, then continue enjoying the benefits. But if you don't, make a few trips with a friend or family member who is already a member. Check out the pricing and the size of products you normally buy elsewhere. Find out if they carry your brands or a close substitute. Remember their selection typically isn't as large as what a supermarket stocks. After you've been there a few times, you can make a better decision as to whether you realize any savings after paying the membership fee.

Another issue is the quantity or size of products. For large families, the savings can truly be felt. Cereals; staples such as flour, sugar, and rice; meats and cold cuts; fruit and vegetables; breads; and canned goods are all incredibly good deals. Sometimes too good to pass up. The savings, however, disappear if you end up throwing away half of the product because it got stale, turned bad, or you got sick of it.

Also consider this: Even though prices on larger packages typically are a better deal, do you need to buy them right now? For example, a bundle of facial tissues typically runs about $17.99 for 10 boxes, or $1.80 per box. The supermarket charges $2.89 per box. Yes, there is no doubt that there is a hard savings of $1.09 per box, but you just shelled out $17.99 for 10 boxes, when one box might have sufficed for your immediate needs. How long does a box of tissues last? And how much longer will 10 boxes last? Probably until after your next employment date. That was $15.10 extra that you spent and didn't need to *at the moment*. Ordinarily, I would recommend buying the 10 boxes because eventually they will be used up. However, while you're unemployed is not the best time to stock up on long-term items because you may need that money for other things. You're much better off buying large quantity items that will be used up in a week or two, not six months down the road.

Also, do your homework and don't get fooled by the large sizes and assume they are a good price. On several occasions, I have seen items that don't end up being a bargain at all over smaller packages found at the supermarket. Break down the prices by the pound, by the box, by the ounce, or whatever unit makes it easier to compare.

There is no doubt that club stores are a way of saving money, but you have to be smart about it. First, buy only what you need. This means writing a list and sticking with it. Second, most club stores mail coupon books each month. Plan your shopping around those coupons. I looked back over the last five months of receipts and found by using coupons for the items needed by our small household of two, my average savings was $8.50 per visit.

Also, if you shop with a good friend and agree to split some of the packages, then you can save money and not worry about the waste. If you get along very well with your shopping mate, you can also split the cost of the membership. But a word of caution: Make sure the person who is pictured on the card is the one who is at the checkout. Otherwise, the store can claim fraud, and although it is unlikely to prosecute, the management can terminate your membership.

Smoking

This section is for those who still smoke and who want some sympathy and a pep talk. If you're a non-smoker, please congratulate yourself on having successfully kicked the habit, or better yet, never have smoked at all, and just skip this section.

If you are still reading on, then I applaud you. Having been a heavy smoker myself, I know all about it: The sense of enjoyment, the sense of shame (especially these days), the sense of hopelessness, the sense of craving, and the sense that you'll have that cigarette above anything else including logic, common sense, your pocketbook, your relationships, and your health. It's a true addiction, and a very hard one to break. You have all of my sympathy.

Quitting is a process. There are usually many failed attempts before that final one that holds. But it's so worthwhile to quit. And the benefits are almost immediate: Friends and family won't be disgusted by your smell; that cough is gone within a few days; your nose will start to work again; the messy ashtray is gone; etc.

The long term benefits are beyond measurement because your chances of cancer diminish, so does the risk of heart attacks, emphysema, circulation problems, bad gums, and a host of other unpleasant and potentially deadly diseases.

But you know this already, I'm sure. So, let's talk about the money aspects of smoking.

I recently asked at my favorite supermarket what the price was of my old brand – I nearly fell over. $7.00 per pack! Assuming that the average smoker goes through a pack in a day, that's a lot of money to burn. Doing the math, that's $49.00 per week, $213 per month, and get this, $2,555 per year! Wow!

And that's not counting the extra cigarettes smoked on weekends or when you go out for the evening with other smokers.

Let's put that in perspective to your salary. Assume you were making $35,000 per year. At a pack per day, you were using 7.3% of your gross salary to buy cigarettes. Tell me, did you get raises of more than 7%? But that wasn't your take-home pay. After federal, state and Social Security taxes, and after other deductions such as insurance, you were netting approximately $24,500 per year. Because you used after-tax dollars to buy cigarettes, it makes sense to use your net pay in this analysis. Your cigarettes cost you more than 10.4% of your take home salary. Let's go one step further. You're collecting unemployment. I don't know what you're receiving, but I'll use the maximum weekly unemployment benefit in Florida; that's $275 per week, less 10% withheld for taxes, that comes to $247.50 per week. A pack per day comes to $49.00 for the week. $49.00 divided by $247.50 comes to 19.8%. You're spending almost 20% of your unemployment benefits on cigarettes. The sad thing is that the math doesn't lie.

I know some of you will say, "I buy discount brands for $4.50 per pack." Okay, let's do the math, assuming $4.50 per pack. At a pack a day, that's $31.50 per week, and $1,638 per year. Even though these cigarettes are a "bargain" you still end up using 12.7% of your net weekly unemployment benefit for cigarettes. Over the course of a year, what do you think you could do with $1,638? How many months' rent would that cover?

And that's not factoring the additional medical costs you incur while you smoke. That's hard to determine, but chances are you probably had doctor's visits that you know you probably wouldn't have had if you weren't smoking. Be honest with yourself.

Spending that much money is bad enough, but to spend it to make yourself sick is even harder to logically grasp. But again, that cigarette craving overrides all logic and sense.

Here's something maybe you didn't think about. You're out of your old job, and maybe that was giving you stress. You are also out of that old routine where you and your fellow smokers used to meet on the loading dock (and freeze) to have that cigarette. What you have right now is the perfect opportunity to ditch the butts. You're out of that routine and if you are a total grouch, it's okay because you won't have any thoughtless coworkers giving you grief. And you certainly won't have any of your old smoking buddies pressuring you to come back to the fold.

The nicotine withdrawal period is slightly under two weeks. And from my many past experiences, this is the toughest part. But it's only two weeks. During this time you might have a hard time focusing or concentrating, and you'll feel spacey. But you're not working, so it won't matter too much, will it?

After the two weeks, the matter is purely psychological. Your body is no longer craving that nicotine; it's just your mind that wants to hide behind a cloud of smoke. If you get to this point, you're more than halfway done with that old habit. Just think, new job, new start, and new smoke-free you! You can do it!

Credit Cards and Debt

Years ago, credit cards were first available for business travelers as a convenience, then they evolved into a way for consumers to buy on credit. The idea was to give people flexibility in how they pay for purchases, either in full within the billing cycle, or stretched over a few months. Using the latter option of course incurs interest.

What happened was that consumers used their credit cards to make purchases, and rather than paying down the debt between purchases, they continued to run debt from month to month. It didn't take long for the credit card companies to realize that they were sitting on a gold mine. Now they had a legal method of collecting money from consumers by simply charging interest. And they are still doing that and making huge profits. Unfortunately, it comes at the expense of all of us who have a credit card.

The average credit card debt in this country is over $4,000 per person. At the current rates, which are about 20%, and making the minimum payment of $100 per month, it would easily take over five and a half years to pay off this debt, assuming no additional charges are made. To make matters worse, that $4,000 debt will cost $6,647. Wow, what a shame to pay that much for things the card holder probably no longer has.

Depending on the balance, most credit card companies charge a lower minimum payment. Using the above example but reducing the minimum payment to $80 per month makes the debt much worse. In this case, it will take over nine years to pay the debt, and the interest alone will be $4,672. The total is $8,672! To drive the point further, paying $70 per month will require more than 15 years to pay off and will ultimately cost $12,893! Paying anything less than $67 per month means that the debt will NEVER be paid; it's less than the monthly interest. This thing called interest is a killer when we are on the paying side!

This is what I call the credit card trap. And most of us have been there. This is when we pay and pay and pay, but the balance never seems to go down. If anything, it goes up because we make more purchases with the card. It's an endless spiraling loop, and it's scary.

Credit card payments: Under normal circumstances, the best thing to do is to stop using the card (or cards), and send more than the minimum payment each month. That's the only safe way out of the spiraling loop. By safe, I mean this option preserves your credit provided you're not late with your payments.

But, you're currently unemployed and you need to preserve your capital to pay food, shelter, gasoline, etc. While you're out of a job, as much as I hate to say this, you should only make the minimum payments. If you think you can spare a few dollars more, then go ahead and do that, but remember to monitor your available funds on a regular basis. However, once you are employed, make it a priority to pay off those credit cards!

That being said, what if you're having a hard time making the minimum payment or any payment at all?

The worst thing you can do is to be late with payments or to skip them entirely. This will damage your credit rating, and because many employers now look at your credit as part of the screening process, you may also be reducing your chances for the better jobs.

A safe option would be to call customer service near the beginning of the billing cycle and explain your situation. There is no guarantee, but some credit card companies may be willing to work with you during your difficult period provided you have a good history and good credit. You may be able to negotiate the interest rate, or reduce the minimum payment. The reason to call near the beginning of the billing cycle is to show that you are sincere and proactive. If you succeed, you'll have a new lower minimum by the time the payment is due.

Another option is to use a home equity line of credit to pay off outstanding credit card debt. Home equity lines usually have a much better interest rate, and the savings in interest charges could be significant. You may also end up with a much lower monthly payment than the total current minimum of all of the credit cards. This option will preserve your credit rating. Unfortunately, using a home equity line of credit will only work if you haven't already hit the maximum, and it's already been opened. Opening a home equity line while you're unemployed may be tough, but if your spouse's salary is high enough, he or she may qualify.

If a home equity line of credit is not possible and you find that you have several accounts with a total minimum payment that is too much to handle, then I advise you to seek professional help with a non-profit and certified credit counselor. One of the services they provide is debt consolidation. Keep in mind that this will lower your credit rating, but won't destroy it. You'll also have to pay for the credit counseling services, but if you've got high debt with high monthly payments, this may be your best option. Just be sure you research the credit counseling company you select; it should be a non-profit organization that is listed with the Better Business Bureau. Be wary of any promises to "fix your credit" or anybody who requires you to pay money up front.

Other options, such as completely ignoring your debt, or filing for bankruptcy are poor choices. Both will completely destroy your credit, and will have serious repercussions in the future. It'll take you years to re-establish your credit. So please avoid going down either one of those paths.

Credit card use: Try to avoid using your credit cards as much as possible; you're only racking up debt that will take you a long time to repay, and you're accruing interest in the process. You're much better off doing without than charging things like dinners, whimsical things, and other purchases you don't need.

You should keep your one card in your purse or wallet for emergencies, such as your car breaking down. The last thing you want is to be stranded without money or at least a means of getting yourself out of an emergency situation.

The recurring theme in this book is to preserve your cash, especially if you think it's likely that you'll be unemployed for a while. I also advocate not using your credit cards. But here is case where you may need to face reality: You need four new tires for your car because the old ones are worn below safe limits and you won't pass your state's safety inspection. You should shop around, look for coupons, consider all alternatives (retreads vs. new), and finally you decide on a set. Obviously, they will be less than ideal, but you'll be able to easily get 20,000 to 25,000 miles of use from them. The total, after balancing, installation, taxes, and disposal of the old ones is $450, including a $50-off coupon. Unless you have a large reserve of cash, it would make sense to charge the tires because $450 pays half of a month's rent, buys two weeks' worth of groceries, or pays several utilities for a month.

You have to be judicious and extremely sparing about your credit card use. Remember, you'll be creating a debt with interest that you will have to pay off once you start working. And you'll probably incur other expenses once you get a new job, such as a couple of new outfits. Other things you may need to charge include urgent home and car repairs. A television set that dies is not an excuse to go out and charge the newest flat screen model; you can pick up a used TV for almost nothing. Once you're working, you can buy yourself that flat screen. For your own sake, don't charge restaurant meals, tickets, or any other items that you don't ABSOLUTELY need. You'll be grateful in the future.

Student Loans: I hate to be the bearer of bad news on this front, but you need to keep paying that one. That's federal money and Uncle Sam wants his money back. If you skip payments, or send less than you are supposed to, you're likely to run into trouble down the road, including a lien against future tax refunds and an adverse effect on your credit rating. Many potential employers also check repayment history of student loans. So, it's best to make your regular monthly payment.

But what if you can't? There are a couple of options, but you MUST first speak with the lending institution of your student loans. According to the College Scholorships.org website, you may apply for a forbearance or a deferment. A forbearance lets you pay only the interest while you are experiencing financial difficulty, and a deferment allows you to defer making any payments, including interest. Eligibility conditions must be met, but you won't know if you qualify until you call your lending institution. Should new arrangements be reached, make sure you get it in writing, and keep this information with the original student loan forms.

To quote directly from College Scholorships.org, "No one benefits when you default on loans." When you're experiencing difficulty in repaying your student loans, call the lending institution immediately to make arrangements. The last thing you want to do is to default on a student loan because it will stay with you for life.

Other debt: What if you have some other debt that you are currently paying? Maybe you have medical bill. If you have outstanding hospital or other medical debt and have to make monthly payments on that, there is a slim chance that you might be able to renegotiate your monthly payment amount. It means contacting the right person on the phone (even better in person). You will have to prove your unemployment status, and you may even have to submit copies of your bank statements. But, if you can reduce the amount you have to shell out every month, it's worth the effort. Should you be successful in at least getting a temporary reduction, make sure it's in writing. Do not take it upon yourself to skip payments or submit less than you should without first contacting the loan holder. Doing that will damage your credit and will greatly reduce your chances of renegotiating the loan repayments.

Payments for alimony, judgments against you, or other court-mandated payments should be paid as you normally would. I would recommend talking with an attorney if you need help lowering the monthly amounts. Skipping payments or sending less than the full monthly amount can land you in jail.

If you borrowed money from a friend or relative, and you're finding it difficult to repay this money as you promised, talk to the loan holder. You obviously were comfortable enough with this person to ask for a loan, so there should be no problem in discussing a temporary arrangement while you're out of work. Just make sure you get it in writing and that both parties sign it. This will avoid any misunderstanding or hard feelings. It's much better to be honest and up front than to take the chicken's way out by skipping payments.

Money Leaks

Money leaks is a term I use for small-ticket items that you buy without thinking about them. When you fill up the tank, you also end up with a soft drink and a bag of chips. On the way into the office, you swing by your favorite coffee shop and pick up a triple latte coffee drink. While you're waiting at the checkout, you throw in your favorite chocolate bar and the latest gossip rag. These are all examples of money leaks. Most of the time, you pay cash for these items unless you add them to your gasoline charges, or on your debit card at the supermarket.

When we were employed it was justifiable, at least somewhat. But, now that we're without that regular paycheck, let's examine these money leaks. A daily fancy coffee is, for the sake of simplicity, $2.00. One single $2.00 purchase won't break the bank, we will all agree. However, let's look at this daily habit over time. Over the course of a week, that's $14.00. Well now, how often do we find that in the streets? And over an average month, that's $60.00. I don't know about yours, but that would pay most of my cell phone bill. Just think about it, that was only one cup of coffee per day.

Don't forget the other things, such as the soft drinks at the local convenience store, the snacks at the service station, or even the newspaper and a bottle of water at the corner store. All of that can easily come to $10.00 a day. Now we're talking serious money; $3,650 per year! And for what? You've got nothing to show for it. If you don't believe me, keep track of every penny you spend for one whole week, and see what you come up with for your average.

So stop the money leaks. Buy your bottled water, soft drinks, and snacks at the supermarket (on sale or with a coupon). Better yet, drink filtered tap water. Make your own coffee. Subscribe to the newspaper. If you must have these things, then at least get the better deals. Convenience stores, gas stations, and vending machines all charge top dollar for those products. Stay away from them, and pay for your gas at the pump to avoid entering the store.

Credit Unions and Bank Fees

Bank fees are one of my pet peeves. It's bad enough that banks lowered interest rates to less than 2% on most savings accounts, but to have them charge you while they use your money is a crime! I refuse to make bank CEOs any richer. Here's how I do it.

First, do your banking with a credit union. As the name implies, the fundamental concept of credit unions is a union of members who pool money together for the common good. In reality, credit unions work very much the same way banks do. However, there are two main differences: membership in the credit union is required, and credit unions are non-profit.

In the past, credit unions had limited membership. They provided financial services for employees of a particular company or industry, a parish or congregation, or some other geographic area. Today, membership is typically less restrictive, and qualifying for credit union membership is easier.

As a member, you are technically an owner of the credit union, hence the reason for limited membership. Members have the right to vote for the board of directors much the same way that stock holders vote for the corporation's board members. Savings accounts are called share accounts and checking accounts are called share draft accounts. The basic principle behind credit unions is to help other members with thrift and credit services, hence your "shares." Because credit unions are typically local and member-oriented, the level of customer service tends to be better than banks.

Lower fees are another good reason to join a credit union. Credit unions are not for profit financial cooperatives. Although they need a profit to stay afloat, profit is not the driving focus of their existence. Service is. Therefore, credit unions generally offer better banking deals to their members.

The down side of credit unions is simple – they are smaller and have fewer branches and ATM machines than banks do. To compensate, many credit unions offer a service called share branching where basic banking functions, such as deposits and withdrawals, can be done at other credit unions. And most credit unions offer ATM, debit, and credit cards that are connected with the major financial networks such as MasterCard and Visa.

One of the best things about credit unions is that they usually have free share draft (checking) accounts. Often they charge less than banks for things like service charges, overdraft fees, and stop payments. Regardless of whether your account is in a credit union or a bank, many of these fees are avoidable, especially overdraft fees.

Overdraft fees are charged when either a check is returned or you use your debit card when you have insufficient funds in the account. Lately, overdraft charges start at $35 per transaction, and two or three of these every month becomes costly. Keeping an accurate checkbook register eliminates this charge. Every time you use your debit card or write a check, be sure to record the transaction in your register and subtract the amount from your total. That way, you always know exactly how much money you have left in your account. Relying on the habit of checking your balance online, or from your smartphone, is not a good idea because some transactions may not have been deducted yet. You may think you have more money than you actually do, but when all the debits hit your account, you may have an overdraft situation.

Intentionally writing checks when you know you don't have the funds is fraud. Checks used to take more time to clear giving people extra days to replenish the account before they hit. Now some checks clear instantly, so be sure you have enough money in your account before you write any.

Service charges are something else to avoid. Find a credit union or a bank that offers free checking accounts. Totally free accounts are harder to find these days because many financial institutions place stipulations on them. For example, you may have free checking if you keep a minimum balance of $1,000 in the account. Others may allow you to write up to five checks per month, or your account may be free only if it's a paperless account. Try to find one that you can live with and close your existing account. Why pay $10 every month for a bank to hold onto your money? Think about it – that's $120 per year; it's certainly worth switching, and in this competitive environment, financial institutions make it easier.

All banks and credit unions must disclose their fees in writing. Look over this information, and pay close attention to any stipulations on your account. The last thing you need is to accidentally trigger a charge that could be automatically deducted from your account. That might leave you with less money than you think, thereby increasing your chances for an overdraft.

Also monitor your account on a regular basis. Most banks and credit unions offer online access to your accounts, and many still send monthly statements. Better yet, take the next step to reconcile or balance your checkbook every month. Your bank can make mistakes, and so can you. By balancing your account, you will find these errors, and avoid potential overdraft situations.

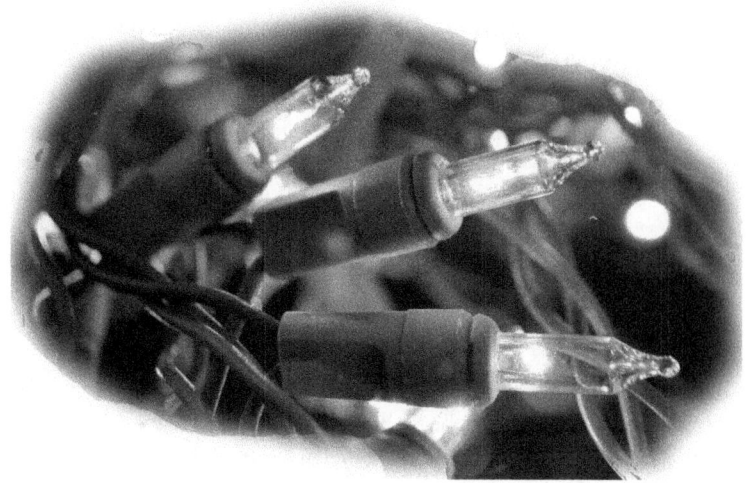

Holidays

In Part I we discussed holidays briefly in terms of gift-giving. But in this section, let's talk about the holidays in general, and how they can affect your wallet.

First, by holidays, I mean those calendar events that occur between Thanksgiving and New Year's Day and include Chanukah and Christmas. In the interest of fairness, I'm keeping religion out of this discussion. Regardless of your religious affiliation, the string of these holidays can cause you some financial stress; there are parties, events, dinners, decorations, etc. So, how can you get through the season with your pocketbook somewhat intact? The answer is by walking a fine line.

We all like getting invitations to parties; it's an outing with lots of people, nice food and drink, and something different from the daily grind. Typically the hosts don't charge admission, so you think that this would be a cheap night out, but when you think about it, it's not free. Usually people bring a gift to the hosts. And you'll probably want to dress nicely. As far as clothing is concerned, please see that section in Part I. I'm sure you already have something in your closet that will make you look like a million dollars, so resist that urge to spend money on a new outfit.

Hostess gifts are another matter. Unless you know the hosts very well, you probably won't have a clue as to what to present them. A bottle of wine is always nice if you know their tastes, and if YOU CAN AFFORD THEIR TASTES. There may be other alternatives. For example, I found wonderfully presentable gifts at a big box home store for under $10. It was a small but beautiful orchid plant in full bloom in a unique and attractive pot. In the past I have found that BJ's and Costco carry a nice selection of seasonally themed and wrapped boxed food gifts, many under $15. If you want to give liquor or liqueurs, both of those places have wonderful gift boxes at reasonable prices. If you give it some thought, you're sure to find nice gifts that are perfectly presentable to the hosts; but avoid getting them before the last minute, because otherwise your choices will be severely limited.

This is also the season for charity events. If at all possible, limit those, and definitely limit the gift amount. This is not the time to make charitable donations. You can, however, offer to donate your time. This may be a way out of a touchy situation where you feel you must attend the event, but you don't want to part with money.

People are more apt to get together during the holiday season, and that includes dining out. My initial advice is to decline them all, but I know that won't happen. To be honest, I could not decline invitations myself. But remember, the bill is likely to be split evenly regardless whether you had a small salad and a glass of water while some of your table mates may have had a couple of drinks, an appetizer, and even dessert and coffee. Of course, you can always state that you'll only pay for what you've consumed, but sometimes the social setting makes it awkward to do that. So be selective about which outings you decide to attend. You know your friends (and their friends) better than anybody else, and if you think it's likely that you'll end up paying for other people's alcohol and deserts when all you've had were breadsticks, then you might want to stay home.

We all know that the markup on holiday decorations is incredibly high. Even when I've had a good income, I hated dishing out money for these things because I didn't think they were worth the price. But, we buy them anyway because they're cute, it's Christmas, oh what the heck, or whatever other rationalization we all use. Keep in mind that if you're unfortunate enough to be out of work during the holidays, this is NOT a good time to be buying imported plastic at inflated prices. Chances are that you've got decorations from previous years. Reuse them, and save your money. Put the tree in a different place and/or rearrange the decorations to make them look different. You can still make your home look festive with minimal expenditure.

This is also the season for **money leaks**, so be wary of the temptation to buy things you normally wouldn't. Just because you're in the holiday spirit doesn't mean you should spend more than you normally do.

Remember the reason for the holidays and keep your wallet shut as much as you can. It doesn't mean you'll not have as good of a time as you had in the past. It just means you're a bit wiser with your money because you need to preserve it.

$10 Mail-In Rebate

When you purchase $30 worth of eligible Neutrogena® Acne, Facial Cleansing, Facial Treatments and/or Facial Moisturizer products. All purchases must be ... 2012 through June 6, 20... Fol... ... submit your rebate...

Rebates

I take advantage of MOST rebate offers, particularly if it's something I normally buy. I look at this as free money: Here is $5 if you buy this. It's a good deal provided you use the product.

Most rebates require you to fill in a form (actual piece of paper or a website), attach the receipt, clip the UPC code, and mail it to the manufacturer or retailer. In four to six weeks, you get a postcard in the mail that is actually a check. Your expense was the price of a postage stamp, so even if the check is for $2, you're still way ahead of the game.

Maybe in the past you were too busy to deal with the process and decided your time was more important than the few dollars. And you're probably right. Now however, you have the time. A couple of dollars here, five there, and the first thing you know, it adds up to real money.

There are a couple of caveats, however. If you noticed, I mentioned I take advantage of MOST rebate offers. There are some that I'm likely to decline, and here is the reason: They want to know too much information about me. Having been a victim of identity theft, I am extremely wary of what personal information I give and to whom.

Look to see what information the receipt contains about you before mailing it to them. First, does it have your credit card number? What about all of the other things you bought; are there items marked that would best be known only to you?

Also look at the form you have to fill out. If it asks for more than your name and address, I would give it a second thought. Recently I passed up a rebate for our dog's medication because I thought they wanted to know way too much information about our household, including income. Keep in mind that rebates are a cheap way for marketers to get valuable information about you. Don't sell yourself and your privacy for $5. Doing this may put your name on an email, mail, or phone list, which is likely to be sold to another nameless entity. Use judgment and common sense when you consider submitting rebates.

Bartering

Bartering may be the oldest form of commerce; it certainly pre-dates the concept of money. Money is a medium of exchange. It has a set value that both parties of the transaction recognize and accept, and therefore money is a convenience used to exchange for goods and services. Bartering is an exchange of goods and services for other goods and services. The problem with bartering is that it's sometimes hard to know exactly if one side of the deal is equal to the other. For example, if someone is willing to paint the exterior of a mechanic's house in return for a car repair job, which one is getting the better deal? It depends on the extent of the repair, but I can vouch that painting the exterior of a house is a huge undertaking.

As I mentioned earlier, money is a convenient way to exchange goods and services. But when money is in short supply, there is nothing to prevent you from bartering. The transaction can still occur, but it's more complicated. If you are a house painter and need a new transmission, and you are willing to paint for the work, then this is bartering. The problem is finding a good mechanic who needs his house painted. See why money is much easier?

Bartering works best between two people acquainted with each other who know the talents and/or goods of the other. The second best way is to network. Your friends and relatives may know of a good mechanic whose house paint is peeling. Third, are old fashioned message boards where you can advertise your services for what you need, if you can still find such a board. Finally, there is the internet with a host of websites specifically designed for bartering.

There are many bartering sites on the internet. Some are designed for companies to barter with other companies or businesses, some are for businesses to individuals, and others are geared more towards individuals to individuals. One that stands out is Craigslist. From the main menu page for your area, there is a bartering link in the "for sale" section. It works the same way as the rest of Craigslist. At the time of this writing, I saw ads offering electrical work, computer repair, and even tattoos. And of course, Craigslist.com is free.

There are other bartering websites such as U-Exchange.com, Swaptree.com, and Trashbank.com. Most of these are also free, but registration is required. On some, I've even seen real estate up for trade. Make sure you read the fine print on any website you use because some charge commissions, and exercise caution. If a deal sounds too good to be true, it probably is. Also, be careful how you word your ads, particularly if you are offering services. You never know what kind of people your ad may attract. And when meeting people to negotiate a transaction, do it in a public place like a mall; you should not invite strangers to your home unless you are offering something large that can't be easily moved. If it's absolutely necessary to go to a stranger's home, don't do it alone; bring a buddy with you.

Remember, bartering is a transaction, and with any other transaction, there is also an agreement to go with it. Most of the time, the agreement is verbal: "I'll do this and in return you'll do that." But even when money is used in a transaction, higher-value agreements are usually written. If you hire a contractor to replace your roof, it would be wise if the agreement were in writing; in other words, a contract. Just because no money is swapping hands, doesn't mean a bartering deal shouldn't be in writing. It's still a contract. So, if you are offering higher-value services in return for other goods or services, put it in writing. It keeps honest people honest and eliminates misunderstandings.

One last word on bartering: Uncle Sam treats bartering as income and he wants his share. According to the IRS website, "If you conduct any direct barter – barter for another's products or services – you will have to report the fair market value of the products or services you received on your tax return."

Some bartering websites function as a barter exchange, where the website (or exchange) will function as a broker. Typically these websites charge for their services and all transactions are recorded. They will mail 1099-B forms for your tax purposes and will also report the transaction to the IRS.

I'm not saying that the IRS will find out about the bartering deal you made, via Craigslist, with an electrician to fix a circuit that keeps popping in return for computer repair. They might, who knows. I'm an advocate of being truthful with my taxes, but I also believe that Uncle Sam doesn't need to know every single aspect of my private life either. Use judgment and caution regarding your bartering and taxes.

DIY – Do It Yourself

I touched on this topic in Part I under the YARD AND GARDEN section, but it's worth revisiting because I'm going to talk here about anything that needs repair – from leaking faucets to computer viruses.

Most people know their occupations very well and we also have a few other talents. Some lucky people are capable of doing much more than the rest of us, but very few can do everything. There will come a point when you'll need to seek professional services of some sort, whether it's for a huge infestation of ants, or an air conditioning unit that had a total meltdown. However, if you are somewhat handy and mechanically inclined, you've got an advantage. You might be able to save lots of money by doing it yourself.

I attempt to do things myself before I pay someone else to do it. Again, it's my nature. But there are limits. For example, I planted some hedges along the sides of our property for privacy. Being in Florida, the hedge grew quickly. I purchased an attachment to my gasoline powered trimmer to trim the hedges. Granted, it took me longer than the pros, but I was pleased with the results. Eventually the process became a problem when the hedges grew to be over 7 feet tall. I had to stand on wobbly step ladders while trying to over reach with the powered trimmer. It would take me the better part of two days in the hot Florida sun, plus there was a huge safety risk. I decided that a fall from a ladder with a dangerous piece of machinery was not worth the savings.

The point is this: Know your limits. Do the things you can, and leave the ones you can't to the experts. Not only does this prevent serious injury, but it may also avoid a worse situation, or some other risk, such as electrocution or fire.

Before you attempt anything, look, observe, and analyze. By this, I mean to look at the current situation, observe how something is supposed to run, and determine the problem, if there is one. Then analyze the situation. Here is another example: A few years ago our garage door wasn't working correctly. After some observation, I concluded that the counter spring wasn't properly set, which would cause the door to seem "heavier" than it should when opening and closing. I looked at the spring; it was in two parts, each about 3 feet long. I could see that the springs' tension was held by nuts, and there were grooves where some lever could be inserted to adjust the tension. So I looked and I observed; I found the problem. And now for the analysis: Do I have the lever to adjust that tension? Those two springs are made of heavy gauge wire and are tightly coiled; by how much do I increase that tension? What would happen if I release the nut holding the tension? The springs are not new and rather rusty; what would happen if one of those springs snaps? What would happen to my hands and face should one of those springs let go unexpectedly? The result of my analysis was that I should call an expert. The risk was too high: I could have broken the springs, I could have damaged the door itself, or I could have been severely injured.

If you think you can handle the task at hand, then arm yourself with knowledge before you attempt. Ask questions at the home improvement superstore or your local hardware store even if you already have a good idea of how to do it. They may give you some advice that will make the job easier, or of a way to save yourself some more money. It's also worth asking friends and relatives if they have any experiences or thoughts, although you may get more information than you need. We are lucky to be living in the information age. With a few key words, you can access countless how-to websites and videos. A few years ago I got detailed instructions complete with photos on how to install hurricane shutters. After I finished my project, I sent the author an email thanking him for his posting, and he responded that he was glad it helped. And last year, I watched several videos on how to replace a sink disposer before I attempted doing the same to ours. To me this was invaluable information.

There are times when the risks are minimal and the chances of injury or the chances of you breaking something are none. Recently friends were faced with the prospect of paying someone to install a home router for their computer, or attempting it themselves. They found how-to videos on YouTube specifically for their router's make and model. Clearly, it was unlikely that they would hurt themselves, and the worst case was that they would mess up the router's configuration settings and would have to call a computer technician. They decided it was worth the attempt. They were successful in configuring the router and saved themselves the $50 to $100 service charge.

Inversely, you might want to apply the "look, observe, and analyze" process even if you're not mechanically inclined. Remember, the process takes place before you physically do anything, and it just involves using your eyes and a few brain cells. Let's say you've come home and noticed that the power is out in a section of your home. You look at the circuit panel and notice that one breaker has been tripped. You reset it, but it pops again. You may think to yourself, "I don't know anything about electricity, so I better call someone." But, before you call that electrician, check to make sure you don't have something plugged in that is too much for the circuit, such as a space heater or too many holiday lights. Looking for something as simple as this can avoid a costly visit by an electrician.

Reduce/Reuse/Recycle

Reduce/Reuse/Recycle is the catch phrase for the green movement to help minimize our impact on the environment. Whether you subscribe to this mindset is not for this author to say, but did you ever consider that some of these concepts also minimize the impact on your wallet?

Take the first part: Reduce. Common sense tells us that for many things, the less we use the less we pay. Taken a step further, the less we use some things, the less frequently we have to replace it. We've already discussed electricity, heating fuel, and gasoline, but the same principles apply to almost everything we use, from paper towels to expensive perfumes.

Sometimes we need to recondition ourselves. We need a clean pair of jeans so we throw them into the washer and dryer with little else. We leave battery-operated devices on when they're not in use. We use three or four sheets of paper towels when one would have been sufficient. Once in a while doesn't make that much of an impact on the environment or our pocketbooks, but repeated waste in all aspects of our daily lives certainly does.

Condition yourself and your family to be more frugal in all aspects of your life. For example, do you end up pouring the excess milk down the drain after you finished your cereal? If so, then you used too much. Assuming milk costs $4.00 per gallon and you dump 6 ounces down the drain, that's 19 cents. No big deal you say. Except on a yearly basis, you poured over 17 gallons of milk down the drain, which equates to more than $68. Tomorrow morning, try to remember to use less milk.

And that's only one example of over use. Pay attention to how much of any food, personal, or household product you use. If you catch yourself trying to somehow get rid of an excess, either by stuffing yourself, rinsing it away, or blotting it up, then you're simply using too much.

When I buy something, I expect it to last forever. I know it's foolish in today's world where most things are imported and are of inferior quality, construction, and materials. But it's my nature; I'd rather buy something I don't have rather than replacing something I already own. So I make things last as long as I can. Sending garments out to the cleaners makes my better clothing look refreshed; I don't have to go out to buy new ones. I clean the lawnmower after each use and keep it maintained to get the maximum life out of it. I look at the care section of the manual when I buy something. I put my sneakers into the washer (not for the full cycle) to make them look new. The point of my actions is to make things last. And that's important when you're living on a reduced income.

I'm also often ridiculed in that when I throw something out, even the junkman wouldn't want it. When something breaks, my first inclination is attempt a repair. I was raised that way, so I've got glue, screws, tape, thread, twist ties, and staples, and I'm not afraid to use them – but there are limits. If something is broken and the repair doesn't show (at least too much), then do the best you can with it until you're back on your feet and you can replace it. However, don't do this if it poses a health or safety risk, will cause your family undue embarrassment (your kids might not forgive you), or if it just not worth your time and effort.

Other things you can do to reduce overall consumption include:

- Serving smaller portions at meals
- Running appliances only with full loads
- Using half the amount of almost any product
- Washing or cleaning things rather than replacing them
- Trying to mend or repair before tossing out broken things

Remember, whatever you can do to reduce means a direct reduction in your spending.

Reuse and Recycle: As much as possible, try to reuse things before throwing them away. A perfect example is paper towels. If you tore off a sheet and only wiped up a few drops of water on the counter top, that towel can be used again for something dirtier. I throw my slightly used towels under the sink for a second use.

Other things you can reuse are Glad plastic containers. They are washable, although not in the dishwasher. I know people who wash and reuse plastic bags. I don't go that far, but I can attest that those people are millionaires. How do you think they got that way?

I also tend to recycle things. Old clothes that aren't worthy for charity make good rags. When I get rid of an appliance or a tool, I keep a few screws. I swear I've reached into that jar of used screws, bolts, and nuts many times. Sure beats taking the time to make a trip to the hardware store when you need an emergency fix on something. Old milk gallons make great containers for used engine oil (which I take to the proper local facility), and the plastic grocery bags from the supermarket work well for picking up after the dog. Most sheets of paper have a blank back side which can be used for scrap paper.

The point is that before you simply toss something out, ask yourself if there is some other use that will help you. Storing things for "just in case" is okay up to a point, but after a while you may be labeled as a hoarder if you get carried away.

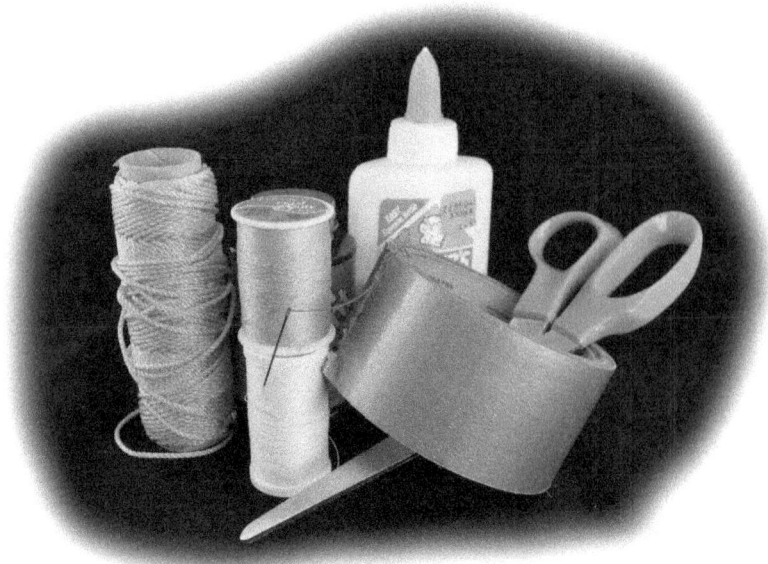

Oops/Ouch/Oh-oh/Oh-no

This is a catch-all section for when things, including ourselves, break. These are never good occurrences even in the best of economic times, but they are much worse when you're out of a job. What do you do?

First, if you or a family member is the one who gets hurt or sick, please look at the section called Health. In it, I give pointers on how to deal with unexpected medical costs.

When things break, we have options:

1. Use it broken.
2. Fix it.
3. Have it fixed.
4. Replace it.
5. Do without.

I can't possibly list everything that can break around the house; there are just too many. But, I can provide ways to deal with breakages.

First, remain calm. Obviously, if there is an emergency situation such as an electrical fire, a gas leak, or any other potentially destructive and dangerous situation, call 911. Don't try to be a fireman or a hero. Get out quickly.

Other things, such as a pipe bursting or an electrical short require fast action. You need to shut the water main or flip the circuit breakers. Whether you rent or own your place, you should know how to shut off both of those.

In the event of an emergency, this will prevent further damage, which would end up costing your more money. It may also save your life.

But for non-emergency mishaps, give yourself a few minutes to think clearly. Whenever I break something or something stops working, my inclination is to go into panic-mode: "How much is this going to cost?" "Who am I going to get to fix it?" "How is this going to affect us today?" Too many thoughts all at once tend to lead us to no particular good. So the washer breaks down and it's full of water and clothes. What do you do?

Give yourself those few minutes, think about the situation and examine the item that broke. Can I still use it if it's broken? Can I fix it myself, even with a temporary fix? Who can I get to fix it? Is it worth having it fixed? Do I need to replace it, or can I do without it for a while?

If you are mechanically inclined, and you've got a good arsenal of tools, do you think you can fix it? Typically, I will open the case to see exactly what the problem is. I have a strong analytical sense plus good observation skills. But not everybody has these skills, or the patience. If I doubt I can fix it, then I won't make an attempt. At least I made the effort to know what the problem is, and I can save the repairman time by pointing it out. Remember, the more time he spends on your problem, the more he's going to charge you.

If you can fix it, great! You came out on top of that situation. But what if you can't completely fix it? Can you attempt a temporary fix? In other words, I mean the item will work, won't pose a health or injury risk, but it's not an ideal fix. For example, a screen on a back window rips, and you know all the screens are old and should be replaced. But for the time being, while you're unemployed, can you mend that rip? It won't be pretty, but it will keep the bugs out. And once you get that new job, you can have all the screens replaced.

So next is this: Do I have it fixed, or do I replace it. Obviously, in the case of the broken washer, you would call someone. Here's a hint: Have a handy list of professionals you can call in the case of an emergency. It can be difficult to find trustworthy people like plumbers, electricians, handyman, appliance repairman, etc. The last thing you want to do is start picking service people from the phonebook or the internet without a reference from someone you know or drawing from past experience. When you're over a barrel, the likeliness of being overcharged is much higher.

Before you make that call, consider the time of day, and the day itself. Many service people will charge a premium for night and weekend service calls. Ask yourself if it can wait; granted it may be a huge inconvenience, but if it saves you $50 or $100 dollars, it may be worth waiting those few hours.

For smaller items that break, you can generally get a good sense whether it's beyond repair or not. But if you're not sure, hold onto it and ask someone. There's chance it can be repaired. The problem is that you'll probably have to pay someone to take it apart to determine whether it can be fixed. That's a judgment call you'll have to make, and sometimes they aren't easy. For example, my gasoline-powered trimmer stopped working. I was ready to throw it out, but I gave myself some time to think about it. The next day I took it to a small engine repair shop. Fortunately, the mechanic had an idea of what the problem was, and he was able to fix it. The repair cost was $30, which was much better than $120 to replace it.

Okay, the item is dead. Next question: Do I replace it, or do I do without. That's another judgment call you'll have to make. Remember, doing without is not permanent; it's just until you get that next job.

If you decide to replace it, try not to be in too much of a hurry. Shop around to find the best deal. Even if it's somewhat urgent, take at least a few minutes to make some calls or to check out a few websites. Those few minutes can save you a huge amount of money.

Retirement

There is no doubt that it's important to save for retirement. We've all heard that Social Security may not be around in 20 or 50 years (depending on who says it), and pension funds may go broke. So it's prudent to plan and save for your retirement.

However, while you're unemployed, it's a different story. It may not the best time to put money into IRAs. And you may even have to pay a penalty if you make IRA contributions when your income level isn't high enough.

The funds in your savings should be used wisely and conservatively while you're unemployed. Putting money into an IRA reduces your cushion, so unless you've got plenty of money in your savings, it's probably not the best use of your cash. Remember, if you put money into an IRA or 401(k), and then a few months later you need that cash, early withdrawals are subject to 10% penalty, plus the withdrawal is subject to taxes. For example, John is certain he'll be getting a job in a few weeks. He worked enough during the tax year to make an IRA deposit of $2,000, so he transfers that amount from his savings to the IRA account. Three months later, John has not been able to find a job, and now he needs that $2,000 to pay the mortgage and other things. Withdrawing $2,000 from his IRA means he'll be subject to a 10% penalty, which in this case is $200. He may now be hit with a tax bill of 20-25%. Now he's only got between $1,300 and $1,400 to use; he might as well have thrown $600 or $700 out of the car window.

Once you are back at work, you can make contributions again. Just make sure you know what your legal limit is.

Speaking of retirement funds, what if you need to use them while you're out of work? Well, legally it's your money, and you do have the right to withdraw some or all of your funds. Be aware that you will have to pay an early withdrawal penalty unless you are over 59 ½ years old. And depending on the type of retirement account, you will also take a tax hit because the amount of the withdrawal may be considered as income.

Taking money out of your retirement accounts should only be done as a last resort. If you've got other funds, consider using those first. The likelihood of you replacing retirement funds is slim, and even if you do, you've lost out on the dividends, gains, and interest. Plus, you've had to pay penalties. I totally understand your point if you say it's your last resort. Just make sure you talk with a tax or financial professional before you make any withdrawals. That way you'll understand all of the implications because it can cost you dearly. I really wish there were another answer. Just try your hardest to replace it once you start working again.

Government Assistance

Unemployment Compensation: As soon as you get your walking papers, pink slip, the axe, or whatever other colloquialism you want to use for your situation, you should file for unemployment compensation. The reason is simple; in most states there is a waiting period of one or two weeks from the time you apply. If you wait three weeks before applying, you may end up going five weeks without some compensation, assuming you didn't get a severance package. So why wait that long? Just do it immediately.

The process varies from state to state. In Florida, it's all done online. In other states, you may have to file in person and then claim your weeks via internet or phone. In any case, be sure to have some basic documents with you, or at least nearby. These would include your Social Security card, your last or most recent paycheck stub, and of course, official ID, such as your driver's license or passport, and if applicable, your green card. It would also be a good idea to have basic information about your ex-employer: the complete address, phone number, supervisor's name and phone number, etc. The more organized you are, the faster your claim will be successfully processed; therefore, the sooner you get your unemployment compensation.

Incidentally, unemployment compensation is considered taxable income by Uncle Sam and possibly by your state. If you have the option to withhold some of your unemployment benefits, please do it. You'll be hit with a tax bill if you don't. A good estimate is 10% withholding for federal taxes, and something between 5 and 7% for state taxes. If you live in a state that has income taxes, find out if your unemployment compensation is taxable, and how much should be withheld.

If you don't have the option to withhold taxes from your unemployment benefits, then please be wise and set some aside. Yes, I know it's hard, but it'll be worse when you're hit with a tax bill. The IRS wants its money and it doesn't care what your situation is, so try to avoid a nasty mess.

Food Stamps and/or Welfare: If you qualify, you may be able to get assistance to buy food and other essential needs. Usually to qualify, you have to prove your financial situation by providing bank statements, paycheck stubs, lease or mortgage information, etc. Do your homework before you apply by having all necessary documentation in hand. It'll make the process move more smoothly, and you'll receive benefits more quickly.

If you apply and are accepted for welfare programs, there is no reason to feel ashamed. These programs are designed to be a safety net for those who have encountered hard times. They were not meant to be a way of life, but that's not a concern for you because your situation is only temporary. You will find that next job and then you can be self-sufficient once again. In the meantime you need to put food on the table for your family. Make sure you ask and apply for all assistance programs that are offered. You'll need every penny to live and to have the ability to go out on interviews.

Training and Re-tooling Programs: Your local unemployment office, in conjunction with state and federal agencies, may offer programs that will enable you to go back to school for additional training or to learn new skills that will make you more employable. Look into them if they are offered. Keep in mind that you may need to make some difficult decisions about your life, so don't make them lightly. If your unemployment office offers vouchers for schools, then go to each potential school and make sure you know what you're signing up for, such as the curriculum, duration of the program, and if the school offers any assistance with job placement upon completion. Also think about how your life will be different while you're in school: Will you need daycare? How will the training schedule affect your family? Will you need to work part-time? Will you be expected to continue your job search while you're in school?

Also, speaking from experience, the application forms require a huge amount of personal information. Complete these forms fully and to the absolute best of your ability. Also make sure you have all necessary documentation. Missing information will probably make you ineligible and you'll have to start over.

Unemployment offices and resources: As part of your application for unemployment compensation, you may be required to attend an orientation about the unemployment compensation program. And even if you aren't required, you should attend. Many unemployment offices offer resources such as free access to computers, printers, and fax machines, provided their use is for job search-related activities. They may also conduct classes in basic Microsoft Word, Excel, and other common office software, plus classes or seminars to help you create that winning resume. Make sure you are aware of every offering that might help you get that next job faster.

PART IV – CHANGE

The Silver Lining

Sometimes, lousy things happen that can lead to wonderful and great new experiences. Personally, I've been laid off three times, so I guess that makes me a seasoned veteran. I'll tell you though, that it doesn't get any easier to be told "Thanks, but we no longer need your services, so see ya." The first time it happened, about 75% of my office was let go; we all saw it coming when we were all sitting there for weeks with nothing to do. But, when I was called into the human resources department and given my small severance package and my marching orders, I felt horrible. In my professional career, I had never been fired, but it felt like I had at that point. It smarted like a slap in the face.

After the initial shock and anger, we did some serious thinking...and looking. We decided that this was a good breaking point from our existence in the cold and dark Northeast and made the move to Florida. We found new careers in sunny and warm South Florida; granted it wasn't easy, but it did happen.

I hear stories all the time of people getting laid off one day and enrolling in school for a new career the next day. Or others make a move to another place in the country, or world, where they've always wanted to live.

Getting laid off isn't the end of the world; it could give you a new lease on life. Let me ask you these two questions: Did you have a job just because you needed one to pay the bills? Did you get an energy jolt each morning thinking, "Yes, I'm going to work!" as opposed to, "Damn, I've got to go to work"? If you answered with yes and no respectively, then chances are the job was not a good match for you, your talents and passions. You were probably holding onto it for the same reason most of us do; we needed it. Now that you are free from it, look at what you love to do, and are driven to do. Is it one of your hobbies? Is it something that may be related to what you enjoyed doing evenings and weekends? This may be the perfect opportunity to turn your life around and do something you enjoy.

It doesn't matter what it is, as long as you can earn enough money to get by and put a little something aside for those rainy days. Here is an example: Mary loves to paint. Over the years, she took a few courses in oil painting here and there, but her college degree is in business administration. Nonetheless, on her days off, she would drive along the coast or in the hills, find a view that appealed to her, set up her easel and painted. People would tell her, "Gee, Mary, you should sell your paintings in a gallery," or "Why don't you enter your canvases in a competition?" She would just shrug her shoulders and not say much. Sometimes she would give a painting as a gift and occasionally sell one to a friend of a friend.

Recently, she got laid off from her position as office manager for a construction company; a job she tolerated, but had no affinity for other than the paycheck, which was nice. If she decides to pursue an art career, she has some options: She can sell her paintings; she can market herself as a commercial artist; or she can go back to school to become a graphic artist. Selling artwork in a down economy is tough, but if she paints scenes that people want to buy, she might do well. It may not be what she likes to paint. However, it would be a small sacrifice to do what she loves. Likewise, if she becomes a commercial artist, then she will have to paint what the job requires, but this type of position has a steady salary plus benefits if she gets hired by a decent company. Finally, she can go back to school to get formal training to become a graphic artist. Again, she may not be able to paint what she wants, and she may have to use other media, such as digital imaging, but these positions would be much closer to her true talents and avocation.

Yes, I can hear many of you saying, "Well I've got kids and need a job with steady income; I can't make money by going out fishing!" or "There's no way I can go to beauty school right now. How am I going to pay the mortgage, buy groceries, and make my car payment?" or "I just cook for my friends and family; I'm not really very serious about it." I know all of these arguments because I have personally used them with my friends and family. One of my passions is photography. I was told "Why don't you sell them?" and "You should enter your photos in a contest," and "Maybe you should become a photographer." Your reasons for not doing what you truly love doing may be valid, but maybe you haven't looked hard enough to find the solution.

Or maybe you haven't found the right angle. For example, John likes to cook. He does all the cooking for his household and decides against a career in cooking because at the end of the meal, he's tired. He thinks that he can't physically do the job. Well, maybe not actually doing the cooking, but there are other positions that may be suited for his talent and his physical capabilities such as a food photographer or stylist, or a nutritionist. He may actually prefer one specialized part of cooking such a baking. Sometimes, we get locked into one train of thought and it's hard to break out of it.

Here is one last thought on how to combat those arguments of why you can't do something you love. Maybe you just haven't found the "thing" you excel at or love to do. Here's another example. For years close friends urged me to do something with my photography, but no part of it struck me as something I'd like to do five or six days per week. I also like to cook; however, I don't like spending all day doing it. I make stained glass windows; cutting the glass is hard on my fingers so I only do it once in a great while. I wasn't finding the one thing that would say "this is my purpose." I have many talents, and I'm blessed with a decent brain. I picked up some good skills over the years such as organization, communication, and analysis. It wasn't until I came upon the idea of writing this book, and actually started work on it, when I discovered that this is my "thing." I'm using my brain and my skills without sweating in the kitchen or getting my fingers cut up from glass. I'm also incorporating my photographic and creative abilities. And all the time, it was right under my nose.

Let me finish this section with these few thoughts:

- Think about your passions and your off-work activities to see if there is any way you can derive income from them.

- Is there a side, an angle, or a part of your hobbies that you can turn into a job?
- Consider the possibility of formal training, or even hire yourself out for free with someone who is in the business to get experience.
- Assess your talents and skills to help you find your "thing."

If you get the slightest tingling sensation or excitement about turning one or a part of your passions into a new direction in your life, then by all means take the time to explore your options. Seek help from books on the subject and even consider consulting with a career counselor.

On the other hand, if you truly liked your old job and enjoyed doing it, then you should continue to seek similar employment. This means that your hobbies were only pastimes, things you enjoyed doing on a limited basis. Make an all-out effort to find a similar one. Chances are that you were really good at your job with lots of good experience. Make sure experience and enthusiasm show in your resume and interviews.

What's next?

You suffered a setback by losing your job. After taking the necessary time to lick your wounds, it's time to get started, no matter what your course of action.

If you decide on a new career, then make your plans accordingly. Make sure you know all costs associated with your education or training for your new venture. Spend a lot of time with the admissions representative to get a true picture of what the college, vocational center, or school offers. Make sure you ask a lot of questions, and whether the school will help you with financial aid and student loans.

Have reasonable expectations as to job opportunities after school. Realize that you may have to start over again on the corporate ladder, but look for positions that will allow you to grow. Keep in mind that many schools promise assistance with placement, but most fall miserably short in performance. If you see that job placement consists of a bulletin board with a single listing that is six months old, you may want to reconsider going to that school. Remember, the admissions representative is actually a salesperson who is under pressure to get you to sign on and may end up promising more than what the school can actually do.

You'll also have to get a breakdown of all costs, not just the tuition. These include books, materials, lab fees, testing fees, and there may be other fees once you complete your program such as state licenses and other associated costs.

Estimate what it will cost you while you're in school. Student loans and financial aid will help pay the tuition, but they won't put food on the table. Keep in mind that you'll have to live while you're in school, and that costs money. Have a plan in place for housing, utilities, and car related expenses. Of course, the best tool to help you with this is a BUDGET!!!

Finally, consider not only the time requirements of being in the classroom, but also the extra time you may have to put into your education, such as lab times, projects, and assignments. Some professions require you to be an intern or some may require a set amount of hours under supervised practice. Make sure your planning covers these additional time requirements.

If you decide to continue with your current career, this may also require you to do some footwork. For example, this may be a good time to get some additional training or education in your current field to make you more viable and employable. You may also have to do some research to find out where those jobs are; keep in mind you may have to relocate. Also, network to find out who is hiring and send inquiries directly to the hiring manager rather than the human resources department. There are lots of ways to be creative and innovative in your job search.

The above are a few suggestions to help you get back into the job market, but it's not a comprehensive list. This book is about managing your money while you are unemployed, not a how to book on getting your next job or changing careers. There are plenty of books out there to help you with your job search. So, please look into some of them if you decide you need help.

Many concepts in this book will help you once you do get that new job. Hopefully your next job will have a higher salary than your old one, but what if your new one pays less? You'll still need to be careful with money. And even if it does pay more money, you still have to manage your money. Even with a good salary, it's easy to get yourself into the debt trap by spending more than you actually make.

The other thing you should seriously consider is that you need to save money. During your unemployment you probably deflated your cushion. Even if you didn't have much of a cushion before, you now know the importance of having one, so today is a good time to start rebuilding that nest egg. There is no thing as a sure thing, and you may find yourself unemployed again in the future. I hope not, but we can't take anything for granted any more.

The easiest way to start saving is to look for automatic savings plans with your new employer or your bank. Either one may offer you an option of putting a percentage of your salary into a savings account with the rest going into a checking account. That way, you don't see the money earmarked for savings; therefore you end up surviving on the remainder.

If that isn't an option, then you need to muster some willpower to stash some cash. To do that, I again point to the BUDGET. The best thing is to include a line item in fixed expenses called savings. A moderate amount is 5%, motivated is 10%, and extreme is 15% or more. You OWE it to yourself to pay yourself first before those variable and discretionary expenses. If you pay all of the variable and discretionary expenses first, there'll be nothing left to put into the bank. So pay yourself first and then cut back on the discretionary items. You'll be better off in the long run.

Also, use this new job to help get out of debt. Again this book is not about paying off debt, but about managing money. Using these principles will help you avoid falling into debt and can even help you get out of debt. Credit card debt is a huge trap, and the only way out is to pay down that principal. Just making the minimum payments will never get your debt paid off, especially not with the outrageous interest rates charged over the last few years. You may need some extra help beyond what's included in this book. There are many books about this subject – find a couple that you find helpful, read them, and work at it. There are also credit counselors out there who will work with you to achieve your goals of paying off debt. Just make sure you find one that is with a non-profit agency, otherwise you'll be paying much higher fees for their services.

Conclusion

I sincerely hope your period of unemployment isn't too long. I know from experience that being out of work is not only disastrous financially, but also psychologically. People think that you can enjoy your time, but most of us don't find it enjoyable at all, but rather stressful and depressing because we worry about money (or the lack thereof) and about getting that next job.

Nonetheless, being between jobs is not the end of the world. It can be a golden opportunity to make a career shift into something new and exciting. Even if you don't change careers, a new position in your same field can lead to new opportunities.

Regardless of the career direction, it's very important to make your funds last through the period, and to avoid falling into debt. Hopefully, this book has given you ideas and suggestions to make those dollars stretch.

If you have any feedback or additional ideas, or even if you just want to say what's on your mind, please feel free to visit me at www.HelpYourSavings.com and leave your comments. Also check out my blog; you may get more ideas from your fellow "layoffees."

I wish you all the best in your next career step!

Michael

ABOUT THE AUTHOR

Michael R. Grenier is a graduate of Johnson & Wales University with a B.S. in computer systems management and a minor in accounting. In his technology career, he managed the computing aspects of financial systems. He has also written numerous reports and proposals. In his later career as a commercial real estate appraiser, he used both financial and communication skills in preparing large appraisal reports. As with millions of others, he has experienced the joy of being unemployed. Mr. Grenier was raised in a household where money management was a way of life. He has always lived a frugal lifestyle and understands the concepts of money. This is his first book.

www.ingramcontent.com/pod-product-compliance
Lightning Source LLC
Chambersburg PA
CBHW051455170526
45166CB00001B/261